The Healing Power of Love

The Healing Power of Love

Transcending the
Loss of a Spouse to New Love

*Gloria Lintermans
and Dr. Marilyn Stolzman*

CHAMPION PRESS, LTD.
WISCONSIN

ALSO BY THE AUTHORS:

The Healing Power of Grief

CHAMPION PRESS, LTD.
BELGIUM, WISCONSIN
Copyright © 2006 Gloria Lintermans and Dr. Marilyn Stolzman

ISBN: 1932783512
LCCN: 2005937787

Manufactured in the United States of America

10 9 8 7 6 5 4 3

DEDICATION

To Rick and Hal:
My past, present and future.
Gloria Lintermans

Dedicated to the memory of my beloved parents, my mother Lillian, who intuitively understood the power of love, and my father William, for his gift of words and his ability to "speak the King's English."
Dr. Marilyn Stolzman

ACKNOWLEDGEMENTS

Gloria Lintermans…

To my dear sister Marsha for your loving and generous heart; for your ability to celebrate my triumphs while offering extraordinary comfort in my pain. To Hal, for your unquestioning belief in this project and for bringing sunshine into my life.

To Marjie, John, Linda, Gail, and my dear parents for your loving ability to provide a safe place during my grieving, healing, and the discovery of new love. To my agent, Sharlene Martin, who, if not for your energy, tenacity and new understanding of our subject, this book would not have come to light,

To Richard, Amy, Evan, Lauren and Stacy for your encouragement and support during times of pain and joy. I love and appreciate each one of you. To Ellie, my dear friend, for your invaluable input.

My heartfelt gratitude also goes to:
Hal
Laura & Sam
Judy & Pete
Joy & Jerry
Linda & Ed
Sydel & Jerry
Helen & Jack
Frank & Michael
Marji & Richard

Elaine & Hy
Nori & Charles
Tobie & Richard

widows and widowers who so generously shared their stories of love and hope so that others may benefit.

I have also been blessed with a wonderful co-author, thank you Marilyn Stolzman for being one terrific, dear friend and writing partner – bravo.

Thank you to Brook Noel, editor and publisher extraordinaire, and Sara Pattow of Champion Press for your willingness to put this ray of hope into the world for those grieving the loss of a spouse so that they might know that there is light and love at the end of the tunnel here on earth.

Marilyn Stolzman, Ph.D., L.M.F.T.

I would like to thank the widows and widowers who graciously shared their personal stories so that other people might be helped. My gratitude goes to: Gloria and Hal, Laura and Sam, Judy and Pete, Joy and Jerry, Linda and Ed, Sydel and Jerry, Helen and Jack, Frank and Michael, Marji and Richard, Elaine and Hy, Nori and Charles, and Tobie and Richard.

For my special friends who advised, pushed, encouraged, cared, and supported with loving attitudes and zeal: Gloria Simons, Phyllis Goldberg, Jo Christner, Bob Bride, Stephen Hewitt, Leib Lehmann, Trudy Moss and the therapeutic staff at H.O.P.E., Marsha Ambraziunas, Bonnie Ban, Jo Christner, Cass Lyons, Natalie Taback and Dayna Vainstein.

To our agent, Sharlene Martin, for your steadfast efforts on always encouraging us to plod on and be successful. My thanks to Brook Noel, wise editor who helped us sharpen and refine our words, and Sara Pattow of Champion Press.

To Natalie Jacobson (auntie) for her memory, intelligence and encouraging attitude.

Finally, to my outstanding daughters Dana and Rachel for the work that they do on behalf of the environment and HIV/AIDS; who each in their own way work towards achieving a better, more healing planet.

CONTENTS

INTRODUCTION ... 1

HOW TO HEAL A BROKEN HEART ... *and begin to love again* by Stephen Levine ... 6

CHAPTER ONE	Gloria & Hal	12
CHAPTER TWO	Laura & Sam	30
CHAPTER THREE	Judy & Pete	49
CHAPTER FOUR	Joy & Jerry	65
CHAPTER FIVE	Linda & Ed	75
CHAPTER SIX	Sydel & Jerry	93

THE NEWLYWEDS:
An improbable love story by Martha Weinman Lear ... 106

CHAPTER SEVEN	Helen & Jack	111
CHAPTER EIGHT	Frank & Michael	124
CHAPTER NINE	Marji & Richard	133
CHAPTER TEN	Elaine & Hy	158
CHAPTER ELEVEN	Tobie & Richard	172
CHAPTER TWELVE	Nori & Charles	187

LOVE LIFE: *Sex as Grief Counselor* by Jo Giese ... 199

Bringing It All Together ... 206

INTRODUCTION

To love is to receive a glimpse of heaven.
Karen Sunde

The Healing Power of Love: Transcending the Loss of a Spouse to New Love is a collection of beautifully and honestly told stories of new, loving relationships following the loss of a spouse or partner, a life-affirming, important next step. It is often within the disquieting yet exhilaratingly overlap of grieving and loving, that meaning once again beings to unfold through a committed, new loving relationship.

We have chosen to share these stories in a simple format, one chapter for each of our twelve couples. Yet the subject is complex, emotionally charged and multi-layered, due to the often ongoing grief of loss, coupled with the simultaneous joy of falling in love all over again. Chapter-by-chapter, twelve men and women, widows and widowers of all ages, from all walks of life and situations, share — in their own words — stories of their life-affirming, new loving relationships and the road they each traveled in order to realize them. Each of the twelve chapters begins with an introduction to the couple, a sharing of their experience, from both the male and female perspectives, and concludes with thought-provoking, comments as "***Reflections***" from Marilyn Stolzman, Ph.D., L.M.F.T., a highly respected practicing psychotherapist specializing in grief counseling, a popular lecturer, and the Director of H.O.P.E. Unit Foundation for Bereavement and Transition, a Los Angeles-based, ongoing bereavement support organization serving the community since the 1970s.

The first couple is the story of author Gloria Lintermans, and her loving relationship with Hal following the loss of her husband, Rick. Gloria has shared, as do each of our other couples, essential facts about life and feelings uncovered during the process of moving forward, including:

- The length of the marriage or partnership.
- Length of time since a spouse or partner passed away.
- A description of the support offered by friends and family.
- Whether a grief support group was attended and for how long.
- If so, how the group helped, or did not help, in working through grief.
- During the first two years of mourning, what was the hardest period of time and why.
- At what point in the grieving each began to date.
- Did each begin dating because they were overcome with loneliness and lack of physical intimacy, or did each feel that they were ready to begin a deep friendship? How they met their current partner. Whether or not they were friends before becoming romantically involved.

- How their new relationship impacted their feelings for their late spouse or partner.
- How this new person is different, and how this difference has impacted the relationship.
- How scary it was to become emotionally vulnerable with this new person and how scary it was exploring physical intimacy again.
- How they dealt with today's expectations of sexuality and how it affected their performance. What their expectations were regarding sexual intimacy. Were they able to talk about these expectations with their new partner?
- What the bumps-in-the-road were in this new relationship. What they wished they could have done differently.
- Trouble spots with family getting along with their new partner.
- The future they envision with this person.
- Advice for others in your circumstance.

Each of the people interviewed for this book took a giant leap of faith as they displayed a willingness to love again after painful loss. Most, but not all, were happy in their previous marriages but in each case, meeting a new partner enhanced their lives. Even when they respected and loved their late spouse, they found life, and love, could go on.

The reality is that the transition from grieving to loving never stops. But we learn that grief becomes more bearable, and memories become sweeter as we mourn our loss. It makes it easier if your new partner is receptive to your bringing up the subject of your late spouse. Good memories and sometimes painful memories come into these conversations; the painful ones softened with acceptance.

Clearly, bereavement group support allowed people to work through difficult issues of loss. In the couples we interviewed, none of them connected solely because they could not tolerate their own aloneness. We can only conclude that these relationships were based on "want" rather than "need." As time passes and the mourner begins to heal, the natural inclination is to reach out and make contact with other people in social ways.

One of the key factors that contributed to our couples relatively stress-free new relationships was their own recognition that the early years of raising the family and struggling to make a living were over. The children were grown, there was a lack of money problems that often played out in the early years as a family was developing. Couples were now freer to be a couple without the earlier struggles that young couples go through.

They enhanced each others lives because they were free to travel, explore, enjoy, attend events that interested them and tend to each other. Our couples also shared a good attitude about life and the future. Each appeared grateful for having found each other. They were appreciative of each other's strengths and loved their new-found companionship, which they did not take for granted. These men and women also exhibited a great attitude about looking to the future with hope and caring and optimism about being there for each other. They talked eagerly about things they wanted to do together and how they wanted to be together as each looked forward to a future with joy and anticipation and continued good health.

It is our wish that you will find *The Healing Power of Love* a book of hope and inspiration for re-creating joy and fulfillment in your own life.

> *One word frees us of all the weight and pain of life:*
> *That word is love.*
> Sophocles (496BC – 406 BC)

How to Heal a Broken Heart

We rarely show ourselves enough mercy when we are mourning the loss of a loved one. Here, a noted grief counselor explains how to truly heal — and begin to love again.

by Stephen Levine

DURING MY THREE decades as a grief counselor, so many have asked me if they are grieving "correctly."

How merciless we can be with ourselves.

Nothing is more natural than grief, no emotion more common to our daily experience. Yet we don't know what to do with our pain, and we never have. We have been told to bury our feelings, to keep a stiff upper lip, to "get over it and get on with our lives." As a result, our sorrow goes unattended and manifests itself in so many ways. It weakens the body and compartmentalizes the mind. We become one part love and three parts fear, two parts trust and five parts doubt. Some doors are locked and some flung wide open.

Unrecognized grief—what I call unattended sorrow—disturbs our sleep and infects our dreams; unable to find our way "home" at night, we feel lost all day long. Nightly conflicts wear out our days. Our intuition becomes inhibited. We trust ourselves less. We cannot feel the world around us as we once did, so we experience ourselves as unplugged. We are a bit withdrawn, a little numb at the fingertips. This quality of grief can slow our creativity and dumb us down. Some of us become compulsively busy, fearing that if we slow down for just a minute, we will be overtaken by sorrow. Our confidence that we can make life happen as we wish, our belief in unquestioned expectations, is wounded. Our uncertainty filters every perception. We live our lives as an afterthought.

Whether struggling to accept a sudden loss or still aching from a long-ago death, we need to have mercy on ourselves, to figure out how to move forward. We can no longer turn our back on distress and lingering disappointment. Doing so doesn't work. When we refuse to acknowledge our sorrow, we intensify our pain and close off parts of ourselves. Often our grief is calling out to us, as though it were a cry from a crib in the next room.

One of the great barriers to becoming whole again is doubt. Because we're powerless against our pain, we think we're stuck where we are and can't move in any direction. Attending to this sorrow isn't going to make it all vanish. But doing so begins to unearth the heart, instead of leaving those feelings buried in an unmarked grave.

Loss is the absence of something we were once attached to. Grief is the rope-burn left behind, when that which we held is pulled beyond our grasp.

Acute grief is the immediacy of loss — the inconceivable tragedy. It can feel like a stabbing sensation in the body and mind. It slams shut the heart and leaves exposed only the rawest emotions.

When Darla's husband died in an automobile accident, she says, "I didn't know what to do. I came into the kitchen and didn't know which way to turn. Everything felt so unreal. It was like I was waiting to wake up."

There is a reason we feel so lost. When we love someone, he/she becomes a mirror for our heart. That person reflects back to us the place within us that is love, the divine principle. When that mirror is shattered through death, we may feel as though love itself has died.

At first there is a great tearing away, a breaking away of every certainty. Through fluorescent hospital corridors, sunlit cemeteries and endless condolences, none of the explanations suffice. There remains the feeling that our loved one might walk through the door at any moment.

One morning, as I washed my cereal bowl, I noticed a crack across one side. It reminded me of one Buddhist master's teaching that "the glass is already broken." And the mirror, too, I thought. He said that though a crystal goblet given to him earlier in the day seemed so everlastingly beautiful, so able to catch the sunlight, impermanence was always encroaching; it was just a matter of time before gravity pulled it from the table or the winds of change blew it off the shelf and it lay at his feet as a scattering of shards. In the same way that "the glass is already broken," all that we love will someday turn into dust. But the love will remain.

A means of finding closure, of finishing business, is when we call to our departed loved ones using the intuitive process called "heart speech" and send blessings directly from our heart to theirs. Meeting deeply in the heart allows us to say good-bye without ever losing our connection. Wishing them well on their journey and integrating our grief into a love and concern for their well-being, aids in clearing the path ahead for ourselves.

Our relationship with the departed is not over; it has just changed dimensions. Keep talking to them, and don't be surprised if you seem to hear them answer. Grief is not a time to be too rational. This silent heart speech may last a lifetime. It soothes us.

I know very few people who are not grieving at some level. Feelings of loss don't go away; they go deeper. Acute grief often becomes entangled with loose ends of all sorts of previous traumas: loves betrayed, trusts broken, lies told and believed, opportunities lost, words spoken that can never be retrieved. Our grief becomes chronic, a persistent ache in the heart.

There is no magical cure for such grief. But no matter how long you have felt despondent, there are keys to locked doors, lights for dark hallways. There are maps to the center of our sorrow that can lead us toward healing.

The first step is to stop fleeing from your fears and try to understand them. I have found that a grief journal can open the conduit between the mind and the heart. We become open to unexpected and spontaneous guidance. The willingness to explore our suffering, to find what habitual paths it takes, moves the pen and finds the words. We continually find that the journal writes itself when given half a chance. As we drive to work or walk to meet friends, thoughts arise, inspirations almost, of what might be written in the journal on its next opening. And this reflection of what we feel and how it might be expressed deepens the insight into our process.

There are also things we can do to feel better physically. We hold grief in the belly. We store fear and disappointment, anger and guilt in our gut, creating a hard shield across the abdomen. It's by softening that shield that we heal ourselves; we can unburden the body and mind to find ourselves a bit lighter and the road ahead that much easier to travel.

Here's how to start the healing: Sit quietly, close your eyes and just pay attention to the sensations of your body. As you feel your belly rise and fall with each breath, relax your abdominal muscles and so soften the shield that is holding all of your suffering inside. Each exhalation lets out a little bit of the pain. When you open your eyes, maintain this increased awareness. As you go about your day, notice at what point the sense of loss reasserts itself and you feel the need to tighten your belly again. Many people say they come back to their breathing practice dozens of times a day. Some start the morning with this exercise for 15 minutes or more, and notice how it produces a deeply relieving release of stress.

Soon you will be ready to tap the resources of your heart; the trust that you can love again, forgive yourself and others, and settle unfinished business. Trust returns as slowly as a frightened child to a dark room. We have to overcome fantasies that life is somehow supposed to be in our control and that we are at fault when it is not. We must come to trust the process of healing enough to open our heart to the unknown—to finally take that next step across the span that bridges the broken heart. To do so honors the relationship with lost loved ones.

We must acknowledge the unpredictable unfolding of life with a sense of compassion for ourselves and for all other people who tremble at the brink of what comes next, whether it's tragedy or grace. And we must know that somehow our heart has room for it all.

Reprinted from *Unattended Sorrow: Recovering From Loss and Reviving The Heart* by Stephen Levine. Permission Granted By Rodale.

To love and be loved is to feel the sun from both sides.
David Viscott

1.

Gloria & Hal

HAL AND I STRIVE TO embrace life's challenges, both professionally and personally, with determination. Although there is an age difference of about 14 years, Hal being the older, our similar interests and lifestyles worked to create a bond of friendship that quickly matured into a fulfilling, loving, relationship that has brought joy and new meaning to both of our lives.

Hal had been married his entire adult life to one woman, while I have been married twice, with a long stretch of being single and several long-term relationships between marriages. I was greatly influenced by the sexuality of the '60s and the modern feminist movement that bloomed during that time, Hal was from a much more rigid time in history, and so, was afraid that he might be very inexperienced in building a new relationship physically, emotionally and intellectually.

In bringing you our story, it is my hope that other widows and widowers will embrace our determination to go on with our lives and will also welcome joy and love into their hearts.

Gloria

My husband passed away two and a half years ago. It was a second marriage for each of us, and we had only been married for six years when he died.

My grown children and my sister, who live in other parts of the country, came to be with me for the first three weeks after my husband's death, not only to look after me, but to take care of the normal tasks that need attention in such an event. My step-daughter and her husband live nearby and, although they were grieving as well, offered considerable comfort. After three weeks, although I was still a basket case, I asked my sons, daughter-in-law, and sister to return home to their own lives. Through my emotional fog, somehow I knew that I needed to be alone to get along in my grieving process.

At the urging of a dear cousin, I joined a local support group that met once a week. It was one of the hardest things I've ever forced myself to do, feeling absolutely unable to cope with any new situation or group of people. Yet, I attended for a year.

The bereavement support group helped by giving definition to my grieving process. No matter what else was going on in my life, I knew that every Thursday evening I had a place to express my pain in a safe environment with others who understood completely. While friends and family were wonderfully supportive, I needed the direction provided by the group's facilitator who specialized in grief support, and the emotional bonding that took place among the group's participants.

There were so many "hardest" periods of time during the first two years of mourning my husband's death, including shock, denial, anger, and depression, until, finally, came acceptance and a willingness to seek joy in my life once again. During the first four months, I was in such pain that I thought I'd gone crazy. And then, up until about eight months, I felt overwhelmed with anxiety over my life. This feeling evolved into a deep, dark, sadness for the next several months. However, the second year of my mourning, thankfully, evolved into a time of rebuilding.

Friends encouraged me to begin dating, and I went on several blind dates after six months had passed...big mistake! I absolutely was not ready and did not pursue any of those relationships.

Part of me had hoped those few blind dates would make me feel better. But it only made me feel worse because, at that time, I was so emotionally bankrupt that I couldn't connect to anyone.

I met Hal the night I attended my last "bereavement group" meeting. I was instantly attracted to his energy. We seemed to have a lot in common, both professionally and emotionally. I gave him my business card with the knowing feeling that he would call, but I had no idea if it would be in a week or a year. I hold a life's philosophy that things happen when they should.

Hal called about six months later and we had dinner together; everything moved very quickly, too quickly for my comfort, but I felt emotionally safe with him and we connected well on many levels because of all we had in common.

Over this time, the pain of losing my spouse had grown softer and the sweet memories stronger, but I did feel a need to talk to my adult step-daughters. I wanted to know how they felt about my becoming romantically involved again, and to assure them that my new feelings for Hal did not in any way change how I felt about their father, or themselves. As for myself, I didn't feel disloyal to my late husband, or feel that my new relationship in any way lessened my love for him. My step-daughters not only understood my need to re-create a life that once again embraced a loving, romantic relationship, but encouraged it. Bless their hearts, for they instinctively knew that I wasn't trying to replace their father or the relationship we had created among ourselves and continued to treasure; I would simply be adding another dimension to my life.

My late spouse wasn't retired, so our days had been traditionally structured. Although I have always worked at home, I liked knowing I had "work time" to myself. Hal is retired and since I'm self-employed, we can live our lives spontaneously; the challenge is not being able, or even willing, to be as available for Hal as he would have liked. My late spouse's personality was entirely different from Hal's, but I found each to be compatible with mine. Hal is much more romantically demonstrative, which I enjoy.

However, I don't compare the two, and so, the difference has not impacted my feelings for my late spouse.

Moving from intellectual concept to emotional reality, overlapping my loving and my grieving, required a giant leap of faith when it came to becoming involved in this new relationship. I was scared. When I met Hal, almost a year and a half into my mourning, I was finally doing "okay." I had a satisfying career, good and loving friends and family around me, a satisfying balance in my life. I was feeling good, strong and grateful for the joy that my life once again embraced.

No longer did I think sex would be part of my life, and that was fine, as I was putting my creative energies into other aspects of my life. While the idea of perhaps loving someone was always a possibility, intellectually, I knew that if it happened, okay, if not, my life was fully satisfying. Well, this new 'possibility' knocked me for a loop; this attraction to Hal was emotional, intellectual, and yes, physical.

Hal wanted sex. I wanted a level of emotional comfort. And I knew that once our relationship became physically intimate, my relationship with him would change and I would no longer be a self-sufficient "I" but a "we." That stirred many difficult feelings, starting with the worry, *Will he be attracted to my body?* It was like going through adolescence all over again, with such questions as: *Do I want to see him naked? Am I able or even willing to give up the emotional comfort level that I've worked so hard to obtain after my husband died?*

Having been single for many years between my first and second marriages, however, I'm pretty comfortable with the sexual world of today. Yet …

I told myself that sex is no big thing … it's only a physical act, pleasurable, no big deal. Despite trying to believe these things, it is a big deal emotionally. And, I wasn't sure that he could understand these feelings since men can be "wired" so differently in this area. And I still missed my late husband. Is it even possible to overlap my loving and my grieving? What was I waiting for that would make it okay? A promise from him of a wonderful ever after? No, that would be a fool's promise that can't be made.

I found myself vacillating between thinking that he just wanted sex because he's a man and it's no big deal, I won't lose control over the life I've created or the ability to make it satisfying—to an oh-my-god, what if I fall in love with him, which at 6:53 in the morning after a sleepless night, is a terrifying thought.

Hal and I went away for a weekend. Not "our" bed or "their" bed, but a bed in a lovely hotel by the sea. We walked into the room, sat down at the table; each of us stuck in our own emotional space. I looked at him, he looked at me. I couldn't help blurting out, "Does this feel as weird to you as it does me?"

"Yes!" he said. That helped.

We talked. In our previous marriages, we had, after many years, reached a level not only of intimacy, but also a sense of being totally at ease. Did we now expect to jump magically into that same level of comfort with each other? Probably. Unrealistic? Absolutely. We talked about it, about our hidden expectations. Once this was out in the open, we felt much more comfortable. Perhaps we would eventually become comfortable with each other. But we both realized that comfort would take time and that it was okay to feel awkward for now.

Slowly I began to trust and enjoy Hal. Or, perhaps, better said, I began to trust myself again to be emotionally safe in a new relationship and so, I was able to meet him halfway. It's still scary, but my level of comfort continues to grow.

But ... the reality is that this relationship has four people, only two of whom have an active vote. Sometimes we're crowded, sometimes it's distracting. He is a widower, with loving memories of his late wife. And that is good. But, did I still need to hold my mourning pain dear? It was, after all, a safety net of sorts. Would I rather be an emotionally pampered widow, or a vulnerable newcomer to love? There is status in being the brave, resourceful widow who looked pain and loss in the eye and said: I can make it on my own! But what if he becomes emotionally dependent on me, will I feel treasured or suffocated? It is so much easier, and at the same time harder, than dating was in our youth when we didn't know any better or have these complications.

Beyond my own ups and downs, our relationship hit a challenging bump when I began feeling as though Hal, rather than being able to move forward with me into a new relationship, really needed me to move back with him into the relationship, i.e., lifestyle, which he'd had with his late wife. Since we are such different people (I've always worked; she'd always been a housewife), I felt that Hal wasn't able to understand my need for my time away from him to do what I needed to do.

Also, we both had fully formed families and loyalties to each. During my first marriage, my husband and I had a "joint" family, so there were never conflicts about time spent with whom.

We have since worked through these challenges to a much better understanding and ability to care for each other's needs. I am feeling loved and respected, and have grown to love, trust and treasure this beautiful relationship that has added so much joy to my life.

I am of the belief that "things" are as they should be, so I look back at the eight months that we've been together feeling that it unfolded as it should have with important "learnings" for both of us along the way.

My family has been thrilled, despite my initial misgivings about it with my step-daughters. It has, however, been difficult for one step-daughter to meet Hal as it brings up sadness over losing her father. But feelings are often conflicted and I know that at the same time she's happy for me.

As for future plans? Being together, yes, but as far as marriage and/or living together, there are no plans nor do I "project" ahead.

What I have learned and would like to pass along to others is to be sure that you have finished, as much as possible, grieving your late spouse before becoming romantically involved. There is a great temptation to avoid our grief work by becoming distracted with a new relationship. And, I believe, that the best way to create a fulfilling new relationship, – one that embraces loving memories of my late spouse – is only possible when we have healed enough to have become emotionally vulnerable once again.

Hal

My wife and I were married for over 53 years prior to her passing 26 months ago. I received enough support at that time to prevent an early attempt at suicide, well maybe not an attempt, but certainly a plan of suicide. The prime example that I can give of support is that in my darkest hour and in probably my deepest depression, my two adult sons literally forced me into therapy with a clinical psychologist. And, at that same time, knowing that the clinical psychologist would be helpful in other ways, as she was, she directed me to a psycho pharmacologist who immediately put me on a prescription for antidepressants.

I hadn't thought about attending a grief support group, but in the early stages of my work with the therapist, she, and of course others – friends and family – began urging me to get involved in a grief support group. As a matter of fact, my therapist was so adamant about the prospect that she initially set up an appointment for me with a local group. I actually made an appointment that I subsequently did not keep, to meet with the director. I was equally adamant in my attitude of not wanting to be in a group setting. I felt that the therapist was more than adequate. She did not agree with me.

Ultimately, because I had disappointed my therapist in not showing up for the original appointment, she, knowing my personality as she did at that time, made me promise that I would attend the grief support group at least three times. I promised her, and when I did go to the grief support group, I attended for two years.

I think that the fundamental healing process in a group, my group, or probably any other group, is that you are in an atmosphere of understanding, a collegial setting, with people who know what you're going through because they, too, are going through the exact same thing. And the primary benefit of a group, I think, is that you're aware of so many feelings that you thought were only your own, which are truly almost everyone else's in the group. We had so much commonality that I think "commonality" would be the key word, as well as interests in the whole healing process.

The first few months after my wife's death were beyond description. They were horrible times of despair and loneliness and I was only able to get relief after the first few weeks when the meds that I was taking kicked in, and, after the therapy started to ease some of my feelings of guilt and other feelings that my wife's death had brought forth. And then as the months progressed, there was an easing of the pain and easing of some of the loneliness, although I think that was probably the most prevalent and degenerative aspect of mourning, the absence of my mate who I'd had since, really, childhood because we'd known each other since we were 14 years old.

So it carried through, I would say, for 18 months of the mourning period in cycles of healing, alternating with cycles of depression; the depression become more tolerable, manageable and less intense towards the 18th month. I still have minor bouts with depression, two years and two months later, but my therapist is saying that I am making a lot of progress.

Dating someone new was something I wouldn't even consider. Actually I did not have a series of "dates," as I was fortunate in meeting someone that I felt I would be compatible with and who would also be compatible with me. Luckily we are still together and that's eight months ago. I had no desire to "date." It's probably due to my having been basically with only one woman, and in love with that woman, for the bulk of my life.

My initial and primary motivation to finally date again was to alleviate and eliminate the omnipresent lonely feeling. That was the initial thing. And, again, I was fortunate in having a partner that understood, and had also lost a spouse. We developed something that was far beyond my initial thought of just alleviating my loneliness. We developed a very strong friendship with each other and have gone beyond that in my estimation.

I met Gloria as she was saying farewell, having completed a period of time in the grief support group. I was tremendously impressed with her farewell comments to the members of her group and ultimately we chatted after the group session. As a professional person she gave me her business card and at a point further down the road, six months later, I contacted her and asked her out to dinner.

It's kind of funny how our first "date" came to pass. I, as so many people, especially the men and some of the women who are grieving, have become a total slob. Not in my personal habits, but as far as keeping a neat and tidy office, I was very slovenly and extremely neglectful of filing. At any rate, I had on my desk a huge pile of accumulated documents and papers and bills and so on. I had placed Gloria's business card at the bottom of this pile that kept building month after month.

One morning I was looking for a particular document and while thumbing through all of the documents on my desk, her business card just *flipped out* from underneath this maybe eight-inch stack of paperwork and fell on the floor. I picked it up and almost immediately sent her an e-mail. Because this was a very new thing for me, my pretext was that I wanted to talk to her about a business idea that she had some experience in, and that I would like to take her out to dinner. I thought it was very provident that the card had seemed to appear on it's own by flipping on to the floor.

First came our friendship and then loving feelings for Gloria. First and foremost I will always love and be in love with my wife and the memory of my wife. Nothing and no one will ever change that. But I have already come to realize that, yes, it is possible to love two women at the same time even though Eileen's soul is in another dimension and now affords me only loving memories; and, yes, I do believe that my love for Gloria was 'meant to be.' Gloria, my partner, my friend, my lover, feels the same way about her late husband. Having said that, I must say that initially I did have quite a bit of guilt, feeling that I was betraying the memory of my wife in having another relationship. But in the whole healing process, I think it's important to grasp the basic idea, and it's an oft quoted thing, that "life must go on."

I'm Jewish and that's one of the fundamentals of surviving after you've suffered the loss of a family member or spouse and that is, that life must go on. And I believe in it. I believe that's the way we are intended to heal. Basically I've now overcome the guilt feelings and I think that the essence of my wife (wherever it is, because I do believe that there is a part of us that moves on to another plane) would want me to have a whole life and not a partial life. I think that to have a whole life, a complete life, it's important to have someone to love, besides your children, grandchildren and friends, someone to be romantically in love with.

I'm fortunate, very fortunate because Gloria has many of the qualities and character traits that my late wife had, and maybe that's one of the things that has enabled me to love her, because it has been an easy transition. There are so many things we talk about openly that remind me of my late wife and so all these characteristics are very positive in our relationship.

However, Gloria is different because, first of all, she's younger than I am. Secondly she looks different even though she's beautiful. She has a profession that I admire and can identify with because it is similar to my profession, and she is a very self-sufficient individual, and that I admire. She was a single mother for many years and raised two wonderful children and all of those things make her completely different from my late wife ... completely, except for the character traits.

Yet, starting a new relationship was scary, I think for both of us. But I think it is something that everybody in our position has to face, that frightening moment in life when you become vulnerable and open to a new relationship. It is something you have to overcome, and in overcoming it, you bond together much more than you would in trying to tackle it down the road instead of getting to it as soon as you both feel comfortable talking about it.

It was equally scary exploring new physical intimacy again. You're dealing with two people that have been used to their mates' bodies, been used to sexual techniques that they've both had for many, many years and now they have to experience sex almost like newlyweds. And that is scary and is something again that once you overcome, I think creates a strong bond.

These feelings did impact my performance initially because I think that the whole process emotionally is getting used to somebody while you're still in that grieving process, even though the grieving process is becoming more tolerable and is less traumatic. Nonetheless, that whole scenario of getting used to a new body, a new person, a new technique can be difficult and yet, in any relationship I think it's important to work at, to be understanding, and be open in order to eventually overcome any difficulty.

I don't mean to say that it is a utopian situation, but I mean to say that you make it as pleasant and as pleasurable as you possibly can. My expectations were to duplicate as much as possible the satisfying sexual relationship with my new partner that I had had with my late wife.

At first we weren't able to talk about our expectations, but ultimately we did communicate what we both enjoyed, what we both wanted to avoid, and I think that openness and discussion is essential to any satisfying relationship.

There was a bump in the road, apparently one that is pretty common to people in our situation. Gloria and I began a relationship while I was still clinging to some very deep memories of my late wife. As I become more realistic about the need to build a future, I am growing out of the need to cling to the past.

Would I have done anything differently? Well, yes, I would not have let the overpowering loneliness be the one thing that dictated my needs. I think that I would have been more patient and more content to let us get to know one another over a longer period of time. But that's about the only thing that I would recommend if I had to do it all over again. I would recommend to myself to have patience and not to be impulsive.

I don't know if my life is the exception to the rule, but I can say at the initial stages of our becoming involved with each other, I discussed it with my two adult sons. The immediate reaction from both, and they were independent of each other, was very, very positive. All they could think of was that they were glad I was out of my depression and at a level where I could have another person in my life. They were all for it, way before they met Gloria. And I must add that everybody in both of their families now knows Gloria and love her and have taken her to their hearts.

Neither Gloria nor I have talked about marriage; neither of us for various reasons have a need to be married, but from my point of view I'm hoping that my relationship with Gloria continues until there is nothing left but my essence moving on to another level. I'm just hoping that I have Gloria for the rest of my life. I love her very much and I know that she loves me. I look forward to building our relationship and being with her.

Gloria has met everybody that I have known since I was a young man, many friends who my late wife and I have known for decades and decades, including immediate family and my distant family, and all have received her and love her. That acceptance, of someone's being able to blend in with your life and your friends is, to me, an important factor in building a new relationship. And, I believe to a certain extent that I have done that with her friends and her family as well.

I would tell others in my situation that when they feel they're emotionally ready they make it known that they're ready to date. If they find somebody they would like to see, then go at it slowly and try to approach building a new relationship in a mature way, letting things develop naturally, that is, not being too aggressive even though they're probably both extremely lonely. Above all, remember that you are vulnerable and you are sensitive to a lot of things that the average person, who has not lost a spouse, is not subject to.

Reflections

Hal brought tremendous honesty to his answers in his self-evaluation. At first he might not have recognized that he really wasn't able to take on a new relationship because of still holding deep feelings for his wife. As he came to recognize that he couldn't find a "template" but a new partner, he came to respect and admire the qualities that Gloria possessed. Perhaps she opened and enlarged a new world for him. She might have fit in very well with his comfortable circle of friends, but she had to be loved and admired for herself.

New experiences of being together both physically and emotionally came to be recognized and valued by this couple. Beginning to acquire new memories of pleasurable events and new places began to make up their experiences.

From Gloria's point of view, she was independent and a career woman. She needed a man in her life that could understand her independence and give her room to be herself. She couldn't be a clone of Hal's late wife.

Gloria comments, she wanted "emotional comfort," and then, sex, yet she thought that Hal wanted "sex" and then, emotional comfort. Men and women often have different feelings about engaging in sex. Many women have a strong desire to feel "emotionally connected." I believe as men get involved sexually and develop feelings for their partner, they then feel emotionally connected, too. While approached from a different point of view, men still want to reach a deeper emotional level.

What a tribute to human nature that they both could adapt and expand and have the willingness and patience to see if they could come together and grow in spite of their differences. What they each brought to the relationship was a uniqueness and "special-ness" that they valued about each other. With that in mind, they were willing to try again in order to deepen the friendship and give it a chance to grow.

Love is, above all else, the gift of oneself.
Jean Anouilk (1910 – 1987)

2.

Laura & Sam

LAURA IS A WIDOW whose husband passed away suddenly when she was 48 years old. Laura has remarried Sam, a treasured friend from college who, incidentally, had never married. Laura and Sam had, through the years following college, maintained a friendship so it wasn't a surprise when Laura turned to Sam in her grief. When Laura and Sam married, within the first year of Laura's husband's death, Sam moved into an existing family and family home, one lovingly filled with furniture built by Laura's late husband, a talented woodworker. What must the adjustment have been like for Sam, a successful television and stage actor? Laura had been married to Paul for 23 years.

Paul died very, very suddenly, it was totally unexpected, and the memorial service wasn't held until ten days later. In some ways, this delay was good because it gave everyone a chance to kind of gather and collect their thoughts. My late husband was from a large family, and while his family of origin wasn't all that large, just a sister and brother, his extended family included many cousins, so there was a great deal of family support from his side.

In my family, my sisters were incredible; within hours of Paul's passing my sisters and their husbands arrived from their homes in northern California to be with me. One of my sisters stayed for 12 days. While here, they helped with all the arrangements.

I also have a dear friend living in Australia who got on a plane and stayed with me for an additional two weeks, as I was trying to pick up the pieces and run the family business. I was understandably a total wreck.

During those first 10 days, every day there were probably 25 people in my home. The dining table was just groaning with food. It was overwhelming at times, but I gave myself complete permission to just disappear and be alone in another room when it became overwhelming. I also told my kids, two boys 14 and 20-years-old, that when they needed to take a break from our houseful of people, it was okay to disappear into their bedrooms.

Cyber Help Arrives

I joined an online grief support group but didn't stay with it for very long because it just didn't seem to me to be about anything except what we were feeling immediately following our loss, when I wanted to know how to move through it, how to function, and how to move to a better place emotionally. After four or five months I realized that the group didn't seem to be about that at all.

The only time I saw a counselor was when Sam and I were getting together and I was concerned about the effect this would have on my kids and how to best handle it, so I saw her once by myself and then Sam and I saw her together once or twice.

Initially, the online support group helped me to understand that I wasn't 'losing it,' that other people were experiencing the same feelings as myself. What I later found discouraging about this group was that there were people in it that seemed to have just latched on to this as their identity; they'd been checking in with the group for as long as two and three years and I thought, *Oh gosh, I don't want to stay here.*

From Hardest to Just Hard

In my case, Paul died so suddenly that it changed EVERYTHING and EVERYONE in my life. In the beginning, it was incredibly hard.

Prior to Paul's death, I was teaching part time and I was about to go back to school to get my Master's Degree in psychology. I'd wanted to do this for a long time and had talked about it for a long time, but for many years of our marriage, Paul wasn't sure it was a great goal for me. But finally, at this point in our lives, he was all for it. I was all set up, had even registered to return to school at the end of the summer. Paul owned a lumber business that was finally doing very well and he was looking forward to selling it.

The plan was that I would be the breadwinner once I had a practice going, and he thought that was great. So when he passed away, I had to abandon that, of course, and go in and take care of the family business. In fact, two days after his passing I had to write out payroll checks. Overseeing the business was overwhelming, especially as I had no real ability or affinity for it but suddenly I just had to do it. Thankfully we had a couple of really loyal employees who had worked for him for a long time that were very helpful, but I had to take on the responsibility of the business while at the same time care for our home, a large house and property, and our sons. Paul used to do everything and suddenly this was "my baby" and there was just so much to do. I also felt that I couldn't fall apart because I had to care for my children.

At that time, I'd already had a lot of things on my plate. I was the Mayor of my city. I was on the school board at the school where I used to teach. These were involvements that I couldn't easily abandon.. Perhaps that was a positive thing since I had plenty of distractions. People told me I was too busy and that I should pull back, but what was I going to do … just go home and feel bad?

I really am convinced that you can mourn and do a whole lot of other things at the same time. Being busy was in many ways a blessing for me.

What was most difficult was confronting the loss of the family unit and the reality that my sons had lost their father.

Sam Reappears

Sam and I initially made contact six weeks after my husband's death. But it didn't become romantic, I would say, until three to four months later. In our case, this relationship had potentially always been there so this was an opportunity to bring some redemption out of a tough situation. I was very lonely and very overwhelmed and needy in all dimensions, but I think that I was lucky that I didn't have to go through my grieving without someone being there for me.

Thirty years after we first met, we found each other again, but in a different way. Sam and I had known each other since we were 18-years-old. This is why our relationship was able to become romantic so quickly. Sam and I did theater together when we were in college and while we never dated, we flirted and always had a high awareness of each other. But for some reason there was always some obstacle in the way of us ever really getting together: either he had a girlfriend or I had a boyfriend, or he was going off to all parts of the country doing theater, or I was off in Chicago going to graduate school, and then, I was married to Paul and that was that.

And yet we always stayed in touch, personally and through the friends that Sam and I have had for 30 years. So there was a long-standing friendship and a lot of trust there. I think if it weren't for that, I would have had a hard time dating. Perhaps I would only be ready to start dating now, two and a half years later. But it was totally different with Sam, since I knew him so well. The important thing was that I could be with him and do my mourning at the same time. Initially, I think it was difficult for my late husband's family and my kids to understand that there really wasn't any contradiction between my falling in love with Sam and mourning my late husband.

A Different Point of View

My late husband was very different than Sam. We had a much more ying/yang relationship in that we were more a marriage of opposites, while Sam and I are much more alike. Although I benefited from much of that ying/yang in my relationship with my late husband, in many ways I think that Sam and I are just an 'easier' match because we are temperamentally much more similar. However, I have never compared the two men because I promised myself that I wouldn't. I made a conscious choice not to go there because that's not respectful of either one of them. They are so different and they each have such an important place in my life that to compare them would be to go back to a limited picture of love that I just don't buy.

Butterflies and More

While it was scary at first to let myself become emotionally vulnerable again, I felt some sort of guidance at work helping me to move through the fear. I had no idea if I was even firing on all cylinders at the time. I just took a leap of faith; I just had trust and faith in Sam. My fear wasn't about Sam, it was more like, *Am I ready for this? Is this something I can really give its due in my current state?* But I felt that this was just a miracle that I couldn't turn away from.

I did feel that the rug had been pulled out from under me with my late husband's death, but just knowing how fragile life can be was a great motivator because I thought, well, none of us know how much time we have. When people found out that I was involved with Sam they said, "That's good because you're too young to be alone." and I'd say, "Yeah, and I'm too old to waste time."

The Sex Thing

I wouldn't say that sex was a tough issue for us except that there had been differences in our experiences. Sam had been out dating for many years while I'd been in a relationship with one man for 25 years. So that was a little odd.

Mother and Sons

Our relationship was fraught with potential for our being ambushed on all sides. We had sensitivities because of my kids and my late husband's family, whose members are very close, so we really had to tread carefully. Actually we got 'outed' earlier than we had wanted.

During the early stages of our becoming romantic we had taken to sitting out on the patio and sharing a glass of wine. One evening there was a little neck rubbing and a little kissing and a little kanoodeling and that was very sweet until we were discovered by my 14-year-old son as he caught us in the act. We didn't want to pretend that nothing had happened because that would have been way too dishonest. So I acknowledged to my son that he could see that we were way more than friends. He was outraged. He said that not only was he surprised, but very disturbed. Who could have blamed him; things were coming on him so fast, too fast for him. It was too soon for him because none of us had really processed his father's death let alone grown comfortable that there was now a new man in the picture. Thankfully my son didn't act out, he just talked to me. He's an amazing kid.

He was tearful when I told him that Sam and I were getting married; it really speeded up the grieving for him. It was another change and he wasn't so sure that Sam deserved to come and live in this house that his dad had built. Yet he didn't act out against Sam., which I think really showed his ability to be sensitive and to adapt, to enter into our new lives.

Also, to Sam's credit, his relationship with my son didn't include any kind of deception, nor did Sam come in and try to be an authority figure. Although we sought the advice of a professional counselor about how to best handle the situation, what to expect was anybody's guess. I even felt a little bad about maybe taking advantage of the fact that my son is a really good, deeply friendly kid who values our mother and son relationship and would do a lot not to cross it. He's not the kind of kid to lash out when he gets hurt.

But We're Not Done Here

My older son thought that I was losing my mind. He thought that his mom clearly did not have both oars in the water. He and I argued; he was more direct and angry. And he was more challenging. I ended up writing him a lengthy letter. The purpose of this letter was basically not to take away anything that he'd said, not to convince him, not to talk him into coming around, but just to say, *Here's how it is for me. I know that you lost an incalculable amount and that a father is irreplaceable. I would never try to compare our loss because we're at different places in our lives, but here's what I'm faced with in deciding to make this commitment with Sam.*

You had the advantage of growing up in a house with two really committed adults who were really dedicated to seeing your forward momentum continue. While your younger brother will never get his father back, by marrying Sam he will have two committed adults that support him and see to it that his life continues in its forward path.

I didn't want to just live together with Sam, not because I have a moral problem with it, but because I didn't want things to stay up in the air, to be negotiable when they weren't. So, I thought that commitment was better than sort of moving half way. And I think that for my late husband's family it was sort of the same way. This wasn't a casual sort of boyfriend, this was the real deal. And once we announced that we were getting married, it was time for everybody to put their opinions to rest. And everyone was magnificent. Even at our wedding, my late husband's mother stood up and gave this incredibly eloquent, off-the-cuff toast, it was quite wonderful. They have done a really remarkable job of embracing Sam. It's not always easy, but they've been wonderful considering that in their tradition they mourn for a long time before even considering getting married again. They're amazing and very devoted to my kids.

One of the hardest things to accept is that I have caused pain to people that I love so dearly, because I really did choose to do what I needed to do, and that's hard. It was hard for my kids; it was too soon for my kids. But I don't know if it would have made any difference if I'd waited.

However, my sons have since been able to move through their initial dismay at my relationship with Sam and forge good relations with him, which is a credit not only to them and to Sam, but to my late husband as well. He was terrific in always letting the boys know how much he loved them and how important they were to him— which made his loss very painful for them, but also helped them in their healing, I think. They didn't have a lot of unresolved stuff to settle with him; they were very secure in their relationship with their dad.

A Glance Back

In some ways I feel like I had a shortcut because I had Sam who was so amazingly supportive and able to help me through the grieving process, to let me sob and cry on his shoulder and talk about my late husband and all those things ... as well as during those times when morning dawns and you feel okay.

In summing up the entire experience, I wouldn't have done anything differently. I don't have any regrets. It's just that it was a tough situation with children involved and the last thing I wanted to do was to cause my children pain.

The advice I would give to somebody mourning the loss of their partner/spouse is to try not to freak out the first moment you feel a little okay; try not to feel bad about that, but try to realize its part of the process and that being unhappy is something you have to move through. It's not a state you have to maintain forever as a testament to your lost spouse. And yet, even though the pain is there, don't resist when life hands you an opportunity to live again, to experience love, to experience pleasure in whatever capacity or dimension. Don't fight that too hard. Allow yourself to release some of that pain knowing that your late spouse will stay in your heart; you're just releasing grief and that's not the same as forgetting someone ... you won't do that.

Sam

Laura and I met many years ago, during our college days, when I was in my second year and she a freshman. I was walking into the college theater one day and she was sitting there talking to a friend, and wearing something that exposed her legs. I said something like: "Great legs!" just to be upbeat and nice and appreciative—the interaction in the theatre department is just so intense so much of the time. Although I am really terrible at remembering exactly when that took place, I do remember that wherever she was, and whenever it was, she just always made me smile inside-out and was one person who could always make me laugh; someone that I knew would be as smart and sensitive as I was.

I was really young in my 20's, emotionally far younger than most people at that age and for whatever reason, even though we could have become romantic, I feel that I was the one who had chickened out, and Laura feels she was the one who chickened out. Maybe we both chickened out for whatever reasons, but when I finally came to the point when I thought, this time I'm really going to do it, I found out that she was already dating her late husband and that they were going to get married. So that was that.

When I found out that her husband had died, it really hit me in the gut, just like someone had hit me with a baseball bat. To me, he was always kind of intimidating; he was a powerful force in any room, and also, while I'm a woodworker in the normal sense of the word, he actually not only built everything in their home, but everything he built was a work of art. He was truly a Mozart of woodworking while I was merely a honky-tonk plucker. I was in awe of him on that level because I knew what it took to do it and I had neither the patience nor the skill to work this kind of beauty.

He was also a formidable force that I had admired deeply over the years because he always was his own man; I was always working sort of within the system and deeply admiring of someone who wasn't and yet, was successful. And I was deeply awed by the way he and Laura built their family, by what they had accomplished, which reminded me of my sister and her husband. To see someone who was so alive and so powerful just extinguished like that was a shock.

My second thought was, oh-my-god, Laura's alone and she's available and I wanted her, and I felt sick to my stomach when I thought that, and so I just pushed the thought away. I just felt awful about it. But it just showed me that feelings were still there.

I didn't make a move to contact her after her husband's death because my feelings for her would betray themselves no matter what, and I felt that would be the worst kind of disrespect. So, while I felt awful about not contacting her, I thought if I do, and my feelings get out to either her or the kids or the family, it would be awful, something I just couldn't deal with. And so I didn't know what to do.

We have mutual friends that went back all the way to our college days and one of them suggested that I contact

Laura (this was several weeks after Paul had passed away) and I said, "I just don't know that she needs to hear from me." But then another set of friends suggested that if I didn't want to call her, to just write her a note. So I wrote her what I thought was a respective, supportive note and I just let it go at that. She called maybe a week later and although I hadn't heard her voice on the phone for five or six years, I instantly knew who it was when all she said was "Hi."

Being "Outed"

When we first started out, our goal was mostly about keeping it from the boys, until we were 'outed,' and then it was a matter of making it clear in every way that I was not going to disrespect their father or his memory in any way. And that I was not going to occupy the authority space. I wasn't going to get in their face about anything,

I love kids and I had my chances in that arena a number of times but it wasn't to be. But I participated in the upbringing of my sister's kids quite a lot. I really regretted that Laura's sons' emotional space had been violated by their father's passing and that there really wasn't anything that I could do to take their pain away. So I felt that I had to do everything else that I could to make it okay. Their emotional security had been smashed and there was really no way to bridge that gap, except to prove to them that I was going to respect them as much as I could.

Now I no longer feel like a guest in this home. In fact, I felt absolutely welcome even when I didn't live here. I would walk around in awe even when there was nobody home; I would occasionally walk down the hall and see Laura's late husband's picture and think, "thank you for creating all this." I'm not threatened by his having come before me, I'm just in such deep awe. It can be overwhelming to look around and see that every physical object here is a testament to him. But this is where I live now and I can't constantly think about what came before. Now I look at it and think, amazing stuff, but I don't think that I can't touch anything.

In a way I was remarkably prepared by life to walk in here because I spent most of my adult life in tangent. With life in the theatre you're never in one place for more than three months. One time I had one job that lasted for 10 months, but most of the time it was two to five months max, moving three or four times a year, living in anonymous apartments, and so after you do that for a good number of years, you learn that the actual place isn't that important. But this now feels like home.

On Your Toes Advice
You just have to learn to tap dance really, really well and be respectful. That's the most you can do, be humble and don't deny yourself and who you are, but our situation is a little unique because we came into it very quickly, coming up against family traditions that would not have supported us had we not pushed it, so I felt the need to be as humble

and respectful in every way that I could. And outside of that, I will continue to honor what came before and who we all are today as much as I can in every way.

Reflections

In general, Laura's comments impressed me as being very sensitive and aware of her children and their feelings. I loved when she mentioned she could talk to her younger son...that he didn't act out, but talked to her abut his feelings.

An online support group she attended, "Just didn't seem to be about anything except what we were feeling right after loss," she said. "There did not seem to be any progression or deeper feelings expressed." That Laura wanted more was legitimate and important. She wanted to know how to move through loss, how to function and move on to a better life. This implies that she was ready to return to functioning and wanted assistance. She did not want to stay mired in loss forever. When people get stuck in one of the stages of mourning, they don't move on. As a grief counselor, our therapeutic task becomes finding the stage that they are stuck in and helping them work through those tasks in order to successfully move on to the next stage.

When Laura says that some people in the online group seemed to have latched on to this as their identity and had been participating for as long as two or three years, she was aware that she didn't want to stay there emotionally, and I see this as a healthy response. Laura didn't want to be a professional mourner and stay locked into the hurt and despair forever ... she wanted to grow and heal, and move her life forward.

Paul, her husband, had died suddenly and this, too, changed the nature of how she would grieve. He didn't have a long illness that would have allowed the family time to integrate his loss. When loss is sudden, there is additional or compounded shock, and lack of time to digest what is happening. A person has to respond to the chaos of the moment and is usually knocked off center. This environment is especially challenging when young children are affected by the loss.

Here was a young widow at 48, whose life was turned upside down. She was planning to go back to graduate school and further her education. Suddenly, she had to figure out how to take care of a business and take care of her family as a single parent.

The fact that she knew Sam, and that he was familiar, and that they had stayed in touch for over 30 years was most helpful. He was already her friend. As Laura put it, she "could be with him and do her mourning at the same time." It was comfortable to get his support through her crisis because they were already friends.

There "wasn't any contradiction between my falling in love with Sam and mourning my late husband," Laura had stated. Knowing Sam and being comfortable with him over a long period of time, all helped Laura in the grieving process. This understanding allowed her to speak, cry and be comforted by someone she already knew. This was not the same as turning to a stranger. They began with friendship and it grew, which is often the best way to establish romantic relationships.

The trouble spots in the relationship revolved around her children's responses. Children and parents grieve on different schedules. The mother may be ready for a relationship while the fourteen-year-old is worried about losing his mom as well as his dad. It would be normal for the fourteen-year-old to be angry, feeling as if it's too soon for someone to take his Dad's place.

Children can become conflicted. They want their parent to be happy but they are also not ready to see their mom with another man. The older son was more direct and angry. The younger son talked to his mother. I was impressed with Laura's sensitivity in terms of understanding her children's feelings.

Sam had to make the adjustment of moving into someone else's house, with furniture the husband had made, taking on a new family when he had never married. He had to fit more into their world than they into his, and that involved courage and steadfastness, and many changes for everyone. .

The advice that Laura concludes with is excellent.

1. Try not to freak out the first moment you feel a little okay.
2. Try to realize that that's part of the process and being unhappy is something you need to move through.

3. Don't resist when life hands you an opportunity to live again.
4. Experience love, experience pleasure in whatever capacity or dimension, don't fight against it.
5. Allow yourself to release some of that pain. You won't release that person, that person will stay in your heart. Releasing grief is not the same as forgetting someone.

Sam is sensitive to not being the authority figure. His advice is also striking. Sam's wish to honor Laura, the children, and her late husband in every way seems genuine and touching as he describes what was created before him and what he came to appreciate.

1. Learn to tap dance, really, really well and be respectful.
2. Be humble but don't deny yourself and who you are.
3. Coming into a family situation quickly requires being humble and respectful in every way.

Laura and Sam are a good example of two special people coming from very different places who are trying to integrate their lives, include and be respectful of the children, and, hold a gratitude for what life has given them.

When you love someone,
all your saved-up wishes start coming out.
Elizabeth Bowen (1899-1973)

3.

Judy & Pete

JUDY AND PETE HAVE BEEN in-laws for the past 50 years. Judy's sister, Maryanne, was married to Pete. Judy's husband, Gene, passed away and then, a year later, Pete's wife – or Judy's sister, depending on your perspective – passed away. Judy is a professional woman and accomplished homemaker. Pete has recently retired. So how do a brother and sister-in-law make the transition from lifelong friends, to lovers?

Judy has been a widow for two-and-a-half years, and was married for 47. For the past 18 years, she has been a social worker, referring the bereaved to a particular grief support group.

Pete was married to Maryanne for more than 45 years; it has been fourteen months since she passed away.

Judy

When my husband passed away, I knew that I would attend a grief support group. But I also happened to be part of an incredible community-at-large at my synagogue, as well as a smaller group of friends, also from my synagogue, who have been together as an extended family for 35 years. They are my best, dearest friends; there's a tremendous amount of love, and our children have grown up together. I also know the value of a group support, and so three weeks after my husband, Gene, passed away, I called the leader of the support group I had referred other people to and said, "I have another referral for you. It's me."

A Group Hug

I attended the group for two years and then went into an 'alumni group' of members who had been widowed for over twenty-four months. A small group of us had also formed from the initial group and we still get together monthly, and also meet every Thursday night for dinner, the same night we had previously attended our bereavement support group.

The group gave me a chance to express my feelings, to vent, to see that there were other people in the same boat. I enjoyed my bereavement counseling because I got a lot of satisfaction from being able to help other people and to have the opportunity to talk freely about my own feelings. My husband's death wasn't a total surprise, but I didn't expect him to die at 70. He was diabetic; he came down with pneumonia and stopped breathing. I had given a birthday party for him one month before the day he died, he was feeling that well. So his death was a surprise and it was helpful for me to be able to talk about how I felt. I knew I wanted to get on with my life and I felt that that was part of the healing process. I firmly believe in the group process.

Taking Care of Business

One of the hardest things that I had to do was to assume responsibilities that my husband had always taken care of. I found myself having to run a business that I didn't particularly want to be running, and although I had been involved in the business with him for 20 years, he had bore the responsibility.

Also, I missed terribly being part of a couple, even though my friends had been very supportive. I'm not one of those people who go around beating my breast. I knew that I had to get on with my life.

For me to have to make that decision has been the biggest challenge, because I also had to make some very big changes.

Shifting Sands

I did not have any interest in dating at all. A month after my sister died, I went to Portland, where my late sister and Pete lived. It was his birthday, and before Maryanne had passed away, she and I had planned a birthday party for him. I wanted to follow through with it. His daughter, my niece, and I decided together that we would go through with it.

Then Pete made plans to come down to L.A., to my home, a month later, and all of a sudden it was a different relationship. In the past, it had always been the four of us together. Before Pete's arrival, I shared with my support group that I was feeling awkward about being with him without my late husband and his late wife, my sister. I didn't know what we would even talk about. So all of a sudden it was just the two of us and it was kind of scary for me, but that didn't take long to resolve.

Prelude to Change

Pete and I knew each other for over 47 years as brother and sister-in-law. Even before that, we knew each other at the college we both attended, but we had never paid any real attention to each other.

Before our careers and marriages took us to other cities, Minneapolis was my sister and Pete's home. As children, my sister and I had been close, and remained close as adults, staying in touch by phone after my late husband and I moved to Los Angeles. We traveled back home, to Minneapolis frequently to visit my late husband's parents, and when my sister and I had children of our own, my sister and I grew even closer. Our children also became very close, and stood up for each other at their weddings. Pete and my sister's children are like my children. I feel about Pete's grandchildren, especially the two younger ones, as if they were my own grandchildren.

Shifting Gears

Making the transition from in-laws to a romantic couple was a gradual thing. We were friends before becoming romantically involved, and decided to let our relationship evolve and see where it would take us. I know I didn't turn to Pete out of loneliness. It was out of a genuine love – I've always loved Pete as a brother. He's been my 'brother' for years. Pete and my late husband were buddies. Evolving into a romantic relationship was more of a shift, but it didn't take very much shifting for me. I knew that I wanted to get on with my life, that I wanted to get married again because I missed being a part of a couple. And all of a sudden I said, 'Let's just go with it and see where it takes us.' I was definitely open to it, and it just gradually grew.

Before and After

When Gene died, I missed him, I still miss him. But he's gone and I'm here. I don't care any less about my late husband, but he's not coming back. My late husband and Pete are two different people, and each relationship is also unique.

For one thing, Pete is the most incredible helper you could ask for. He is a warm, caring human being. When we used to visit him and my sister, wherever they lived, I called him Mr. Clean. He's marvelous. My husband never helped me in the house, so I appreciate it. It's not that my husband wasn't kind, but its incredible how helpful Pete is. Pete and I had known each other for a long time, had a history together, but even so, it was scary to allow myself to become emotionally vulnerable again, Even though I knew from the very beginning that I wanted to remarry.

Physically Speaking

I was so used to being with my husband that it was scary even when Pete asked me out just on a friendship basis. We had remained good friends, but I was very scared about going out with Pete. And it ended up that it was a very comfortable evening. In the past, we had always been out as part of a group.

Physical intimacy is, of course, part of our new relationship, and expectations today are far different from when I was first married. When you're younger, I think that you're more willing to take risks. I didn't want to spend the rest of my life alone, but the risk, the unknown, is scary for me. Eventually, I was able to overcome my misgivings and it just kind of happened …. a HELLLLO! kind of thing. It was a beautiful realization and I feel we are both lucky to have this relationship. As our relationship progressed, I decided to talk to my rabbi about it. His response was encouraging and affirmative and I consider myself very fortunate, very lucky.

Is Geography Destiny?

Not everything has been easy. The problem is that Pete currently lives a thousand miles away in Portland, and we're doing the very best that we can. Our bump in the road is that things are a lot different when you're 70 years old instead of in your twenties. Pete and I both come with baggage. He has a father, 97, who is in a home for the aged in Portland. His daughter lives there and is getting married next year, and his son lives in a city nearby. So Pete has his community in Oregon and I have my children and my community in California. The logistics aren't as easy as when you're just starting out and all you have to do is drive across the bridge between Minneapolis and St. Paul as Gene and I did. Still, I don't wish that I had done things any differently.

Family Ties

Instead of facing family opposition, Pete and I experienced just the opposite – support. When the children were growing up and we'd spend summer vacations together, the kids came up with the idea of calling us Auntie Mommy and Uncle Daddy. When we decided it was time to tell the children about our new relationship, the first thing that came out of my youngest son's mouth was, "Uncle Daddy." My kids are thrilled. My grandchildren loved Pete before, and they adore him now. My daughter calls Pete for advice, and Pete's daughter calls me. It's been family all their lives and its family again. They don't know what it's like not having an Uncle Pete in their lives. And I also feel that Pete's kids love me. No question. I don't feel like I'm being disloyal to my late husband because of my relationship with Pete, and my kids don't feel they're being disloyal to their late father. Their father's gone.

My sister had battled cancer for two years. She died in February, and the previous Thanksgiving, I had visited her in Portland, spending a week during which we talked openly with each other. She told me at Thanksgiving that she wanted Pete to get married again after she was gone. We talked a lot, and I feel that God gave us a gift of that whole week together. We loved each other, my sister and I.

Crystal Ball

I foresee a future together with Pete; we will be getting married. For now, I travel to Pete's home, and Pete to mine. Once the logistics can be worked out, we'll get married and I see a wonderful future in front of us. I will soon be out from under the business my late husband and I owned, and I envision myself and Pete as a couple, involved with friends and the community, and spending time traveling, which we both enjoy. We'll live in my house in L.A.. If it had to be I would move to Oregon, but Pete has indicated that he would make the move. He's a very kind person, and very thoughtful.

Although things are working well for myself and Pete, I'm reluctant to offer advice to others. I can't say, don't be afraid. But I do tell people to let yourself feel. Don't hide or be afraid of getting involved in another relationship. Go on with your life; your husband or wife is not coming back. Date. At least date. And don't be afraid, to stick up for your own values, for what matters to you, without being selfish. It was important for me to choose a man of my religion, one who could accept me as a woman with strong viewpoints and one who would accept me for who I am. Don't say, "I'm not going to date." I see widows and widowers doing that, and life is too short.

Pete

My late wife died of cancer, and had been ill for about two years. It was tough knowing there was only one end possible. Family and friends stood by, but this situation was not parallel to Judy's.

I had somewhat of an infrastructure in place, as Judy did. But my career had taken me to many different parts of the country, and because we moved often and hadn't spent a long time in any one community, we didn't develop a large base of lifelong friends, although we did make friendships here and there as we progressed through life. After I retired in 1997, my late wife, Maryanne, and I moved back to Portland, where we had once lived, and built a life within our religious community and with a group of close friends. That group and some other friends were a major source of support when things started to go bad as Maryanne's illness progressed and she subsequently died.

After she passed away I felt that I didn't want to unburden myself completely, preferring to hold back my feelings. But in retrospect, I believe that my friends helped a great deal by keeping me occupied and assuring me that they were there if I needed their help. Although I was moving forward in my grieving, I tend to be a private person and was inclined to wear grief as a badge. I felt I needed to handle this a little bit on my own.

I attended a grief support group, but it was for people suffering from a variety of losses, not exclusively the loss of a partner. I feel that all grief is not the same, or at least not in the way we experience it. Grief is not the same when it comes to loss of a spouse, and I didn't feel I got as much out of the group as I might have if it been made up entirely of people who were in similar circumstances. For about three months, I attended various groups, but would shortly stop going, often drifting away because of the extreme behavior of some of the participants. I thought – Why do I have to go through this when I'm not getting enough out of it to warrant continuing. I did get something out of it, but ... At the same time, I did begin to feel stronger in terms of moving along, and that, too, may have been an important factor in leaving the groups behind.

Answering the Call
Without a doubt, it was Judy, and the fact that she had already gone through the grief of losing her husband, that helped heal my grief. Judy knew what I was going through, and gave me a safe space to mourn. I don't think that I would have advanced nearly so quickly in terms of healing were it not for the development of my relationship with Judy.

The beginning stages of loss were the hardest, and getting used to the idea that my wife was not going to be there. Losing a life partner and the thought of continuing on without her was a daunting task. But at the same time, because she had been ill so long, I felt I had had a chance to prepare myself. Maryanne and I had even talked about this. As things began to unfold, she accepted that I would not go on alone, and it didn't take very long for me to put aside some of these sad feelings. However, I still become teary eyed talking about Maryanne and remembering those parting months. I'm not sure that this would have unfolded exactly in the same way if it hadn't been for my sudden realization that Judy is such a great person.

Even before Maryanne died, Judy was a solid source of support. It further developed into a feeling of great appreciation, and as time passed, I began to get these thoughts, now here's a wonderful woman, and maybe someone I can get closer to. As events unfolded and we began discussing our feeling, the relationship began to change and develop, and it's still developing.

A Sea of Change

Our current relationship developed over a period of time; it wasn't a long period of time, but I had the same apprehensions as Judy about being two when we had always been four. How was that going to work? We were both single, and it was certainly a different relationship. By that time, thoughts about seeing Judy in a whole new way had begun percolating in my mind. But I really wasn't completely ready to let these feelings surface. It wasn't until the end of that first trip to L.A. that we finally were able to begin talking in some depth about each other and our relationship. That was a very interesting and productive time that we spent together. And even though they were sisters, Judy and my late wife, Maryanne, were not alike.

I can't remember the way that Maryanne and I developed our relationship early on. But Maryanne was Maryanne, and Judy is Judy, and they're different. I was unsure about how I should proceed. But time took very good care of that, and obviously, I began to feel much more sure of myself.

Allowing myself to become emotionally vulnerable wasn't exactly frightening, but I was unsure of myself and then, there was sexual intimacy to consider, too.

I felt that intimacy was going to be part of any normal relationship, but you know it's just one of many things that we would work out together. Maryanne and I been together a long time and had developed a level of sexual comfort with each other, so this was something that I wanted to have again, but I knew it would take time to get there and I was willing to give it that.

Hit the Brakes?

I did have concerns, however. If anything, what troubled me most was that this relationship was unfolding so quickly after Maryanne had passed, only three or four months. And maybe it was more of a concern about how this relationship would be perceived by other people than the fact that it actually bothered me. She and I talked about this, about my concern, and we struggled with it. The fact that Judy had discussed it with her rabbi and had received encouragement also helped. I began to feel more comfortable after that. I felt no guilt over it myself, and would not have done anything any differently.

All in the Family

Thankfully I had no problem finding family support for this new relationship. Quite the opposite. My son, who is probably less emotional than my daughter, didn't express himself, but my daughter has been absolutely ecstatic about how this has unfolded. Judy has been just like her mother and she feels tremendously grateful to be able to call on her in moments when she feels that a mother's advice is important.

And Now?

I'm just as pragmatic as Judy is on the subject of our spouses. They are gone, and it is sad that it had to happen the way it did. They died too young, and that's not normal. I feel I still have a life to live and want to make the most of it. It's wonderful that we found each other in this new way. My advice to others is to go on living, and to try to form a new romantic relationship. I'm just not one to resign myself to jumping into the grave with my wife. For your own mental health and physical well-being, you need to get back to normal living.

Reflections

Judy and Pete have a unique situation in that they knew each other before as family. There already was a familiarity and a sweetness in that. What I am touched with in their story is the sincerity of two people who want to explore a life together. Having known each other for a long time, it is comfortable, their families know each other, and their grandchildren have met and know each other.

What the couple calls "baggage" is often part of modern society. A daughter lives here, a son lives there .... it is harder to get together for Sunday dinner. Airplanes become the modern bridge for finding each other and celebrating together, something all of us do. Our families may be an airplane ride away, but our hearts are in the same cities. Living in different states mean someone has to compromise and move to a place that's comfortable for both.

Summer vacations with "Auntie Mommy and Uncle Daddy" are something that the children were used to while growing up. Yet, there still has to be an inner adjustment: "Your mom is doing what with my father?" That adjustment comes with time. All loving, caring . families hope and want their loved ones to be happy, they may not see or feel the nuances till later ... and that doesn't mean it's bad ... it just means it might be different.

Pete has been widowed for 14 months and may need more time to process what has happened to him and how he feels about his loss, even though he would like his life to go forward. A verbalized difference might be that "Judy is ready to move forward but she shares her feelings and Pete wears his grief as a badge." Judy attended a group specifically for widows and widowers while Pete did not. That can make a major difference. There are different issues, and all support groups are not the same, in their depth and in the competence of the professionals running the programs. It is my biased belief that widows and widowers should only be with widows and widowers and that all losses cannot be grouped together because there are different issues.

Judy knew what Pete was going through and gave him a safe place to mourn. She understood about mourning and gave him space.

Here you have a couple coming together who know each other and recognize each other's strengths. They had to overcome the roles they had in the family. Judy sought the counsel of her clergy to explore these issues; which I see as a healthy sign. Judy expressed that she wanted to go on with her life and marry again. "A safe place to mourn" might be a key phrase in which we recognize each other's needs as well as our own when we seek the blessing of community.

Timing is always sensitive to where one is in his process and Pete had concerns about how this relationship would be perceived by others. It might be wise to be sensitive to possible future fallout from Pete's children, although they love Judy. Hidden resentments might emerge as they still grieve the loss of their mother. Judy is an extremely sensitive, caring human being with great awareness. She strikes me as someone who will stay attuned to the nuances of the families' emerging feelings and will be able to work with it. Here are two people, glad they found each other, and happy to participate in each others' lives as meaningful partners with an awareness and deep appreciation of family. The attitude of going forward, making progress, loving and moving on is alive and present.

What we need to know about loving is no great mystery. We all know what constitutes loving behavior; we need but act upon it, not continually question it. Over-analysis often confuses the issue and in the end brings us no closer to insight. We sometimes become too busy classifying, separating, and examining, to remember that love is easy. It's we who make it complicated.

Leo Buscaglia

4.

Joy & Jerry

A TALL MAN with brown hair, Jerry is in contrast to blonde, blue-eyed Joy. They are a handsome couple, obviously devoted to each other.

What is particularly poignant is that a few years ago, Joy was very ill with spinal meningitis and credits Jerry with having saved her life. "He found me unconscious, called my doctor and then, rushed me to the emergency room and hospital." Joy spent a month in the hospital. Although a close couple at that time, Jerry's care during Joy's illness drew them even closer.

In turn, Jerry had a knee replaced nine months ago, and then, recently learned that he had lymphoma of the eye. He has been treated with chemotherapy and will have radiation shortly. They have lovingly supported each other through their illnesses, grateful and delighted that they found one another. They each enthusiastically say, "I want to spend the rest of my life with him/her," respectfully. Joy truly has an infectious gleam in her eye when she talks about Jerry.

Joy has been a widow for four-and-a-half years and was married for 48. Jerry has been a widower for four years.

Joy

My friends and family were there for me at all times. When my husband passed away we were in the process of moving into a new condo. My family and friends were extremely supportive; they helped me unpack, organize the condo, even put things away in the kitchen. At first they came every day, but in time, less and less. They had to get back to their own lives.

After hearing of a bereavement support group that met once a week, I finally joined two months after I became a widow. Finding other people in the same position was comforting and I attended for two years. Not only did I make new friends from within this group, but found a kind of support otherwise missing in my life.

I found the other women in the group welcoming and was grateful when, the first night I attended, they asked if I would like to meet with them for dinner before our weekly group session. Since my husband passed away, more often than not, I had been eating alone and welcomed the company of like women.

A Match-Making Computer
The hardest time for me during the first two years was driving to and from the bereavement support group by myself. I was so lonely that I would often break down in tears while driving.

A year passed before I started dating again. It wasn't loneliness or lack of physical intimacy that prompted this decision. Although I had been asked out a few times by various men, I hadn't felt ready to date. I waited until meeting a man I wanted to get to know better, and that was Jerry. I just knew in my heart that he was someone I would be comfortable with and the bonus was having friends in common. I had a new computer. Jerry kindly mentioned that if I was having trouble with it, he would be glad to help me with it. And the rest is history.

The Next Level
I met Jerry while out for dinner with friends from my bereavement support group. After being introduced, Jerry said he thought we might have some mutual friends. I was a little bit shy, but was drawn to him immediately.

I'm positive that my late husband would be very happy that I am with someone like Jerry, an exceptionally kind, very considerate and likeable person.

Jerry is similar in a lot of ways to my late husband in that they are both kind men, but Jerry is much more socially active. Jerry is somebody who likes to go out a lot – almost every night. My husband was content to stay home doing book work or whatever he had to do.

Becoming emotionally vulnerable was scary with a capital "S." I found myself constantly second-guessing myself: "Gee, am I really supposed to be doing this – kissing or hugging? And then my thoughts would go even deeper, questioning whether I was even supposed to be having these feelings about another man. I also worried about how my kids would react.

Moving ahead, exploring physical intimacy was another challenge. It was scary, but in time it also felt right. I was comfortable with my own expectations of sexuality regardless of the world around me. To me, sex is something that just comes naturally.

Although I had been married to my late husband far longer than Jerry to his late wife, my husband had been sick for a number of years, so sex was something we let go of, but not emotional intimacy, thank god. So, to me, sex was something new all over again. It helped when Jerry admitted that he was nervous and we could share our feelings about becoming physically intimate with someone new.

I'd Like You to Meet …
My son, his wife and children live in Chicago. Jerry and I had known each other a few months when I went there on a visit and Jerry would call on the phone. Although I'd already told them about Jerry, when he called, my son gave

me the third-degree: '*Who* is this guy?' My son was naturally very protective of me; he sort of took on the father role. So I cautioned Jerry not to call so much. I would call him on my cell phone instead, wanting to keep my son from pressuring me with questions I didn't have answers to yet. My older daughter took an instant liking to him. My other son came to meet him in California where we live and liked him very much too. Eventually, Jerry came to Chicago and met the entire family.

Good Vibrations
I don't really think there was a lot we would do differently in the way our families met. Jerry invited his step-son and daughter and their families to a Chinese restaurant wanting us to meet pretty quickly. All in all, it was fairly easy.

I hope to spend the rest of my life with this person, living together or however we decide to be together. My advice to others? Take your time, go easy, *and enjoy* the moment.

Jerry

This had been a second marriage for my late wife, Raye, and me. I had previously been married for 37 years and single for two years when I met and married Raye. Our marriage lasted 13 years before her death. Afterward, I had tremendous support from both family and friends. I also meet people easily and that proved helpful. I attended a bereavement support group for two years, a group in which my late wife had been a facilitator. I found attending the group necessary but challenging.

At each meeting people reacted differently according to where they were in their lives. Some seemed hopeless and, it appeared to me, stubbornly refused to move on. As I continued to go and meet more positive people, I came to look forward to those weekly meetings. Each week became better, warmer, as we drew closer, listening to each other's 'story'. We cared for one another, handing the Kleenex box back and forth. It became like a second family, as time went on.

The hardest times were the first months following my wife's death; the emptiness, the shock, the newness. Gradually, feelings eased, and the group became a source of social interaction as well as support. Within our group, we started to have little parties and get-togethers after about nine months of grieving.

Getting Fixed Up

Friends and family bent over backwards with invitations to movies and dinner. At one point, during one of these occasions, I remember looking out the window and thinking to myself, 'What am I doing with these old fogies'? I quickly realized that I was missing intimate companionship, love. I was ready to move on with my life. It was time to do something about the loneliness and lack of physical intimacy I felt. I was ready to develop a deeper friendship with a woman.

I met Joy at a restaurant. The amazing coincidence was that friends had been telling me that when I was ready to meet someone, they knew someone who they felt would be perfect—Joy!

First, we became friends. I was the person who helped her with computer skills. We would work on the computer and then we would have dinner. Our relationship just evolved from there.

Then and Now

Some old feelings for Raye remain, however. We had a very good relationship, I remember the good times. It doesn't go away. It is there in a special spot in my heart and my head.

Raye and Joy are different in appearance, but have other traits in common. Joy's a little taller and she's blonde. My late wife was a brunette. But their personalities are very similar. Both have a good sense of humor and are women of the world. Both have been active in social, community, charitable endeavors and events. They are women that are out and about.

At the moment, we are living together in Joy's house. She is the best thing that ever happened to me and we seem to be fulfilling all kinds of emotional needs and feelings. Honestly, I can't wait to get home at the end of the day to see her.

To reach this level of emotional and physical intimacy, we certainly had to cross some new bridges. Everything is new because the person is new. But I quickly

began to think ahead to *where are we going with this?*
Ultimately, I felt I would like to spend the rest of my life
with this woman.

The Sex Thing

The thought of exploring physical intimacy again was scary
but not insurmountable ... doing things you thought you
would never do again. It helped that I was somewhat able
to talk about my expectations with Joy. In the beginning it
was difficult; as time went on it got better. My
expectations were to have normal intimacy.

And, equally important, I was able to be myself,
without being intimidated by today's standards of
sexuality. I did the best that I could. I don't think it
affected performance at all.

Not all Roses

Before getting to the happy place that we're at now, we
did encounter a few thorns. Men usually aren't as neat as
women would like us to be, so when we started living
together that came up. Naturally she had her way of
running her place – I respected that, so, perhaps, a little
glitch here and there, but nothing horrible.

Regrets? I would have liked to become closer sooner.

And apprehensions about family acceptance were
needless. If there was any trouble, it was only in my
perception of possible trouble. My family has accepted Joy
and visa-versa. I am the 'Grandpa' to our combined six
grandchildren.

I envision our being together forever. I have a home which I ultimately want to sell, but it needs a lot of cleanup before the house and contents could be sold. We have talked loosely about Joy selling her place so that we can buy a place together.

To the Wise

If you see somebody you like and you have feelings for them, go for it. Ask them out for a drink, get to know them.

Reflections

Jerry was in the photography business and had a wife who was a therapist. Joy's husband was in the clothing business and she worked briefly as a medical assistant. Later, she helped her late husband in his business. In each of their previous relationships, Joy and Jerry had experienced many loving, partnered years.

It was evident when talking with them that they deeply care about each other, evidenced by a great deal of respect. They are a very special couple who openly delight in each other's company. They seem genuinely appreciative that they have found each other. Joy related to me that when she first went out with Jerry, she was nervous and asked her friends, "What should I do?" They said: Buy some eggplant and crackers and a bottle of wine.

On that first date, Jerry wanted to come earlier than the time that had been set. Joy said she was not quite ready and stalled him. He came early anyway, and perhaps this was an early indication of Joy versus Jerry's readiness for a new relationship.

Part of the reason that Jerry and Joy can appreciate each other so much is that both had enjoyed positive past relationships and wanted that again. They value each other and are caring in each other's presence. Each had the opportunity to give a lot to the other at a time when both were ill. This deepened their commitment and love. They each value what the other has given them and are open about sharing their gratitude. Jerry and Joy strike me as a couple who do not take their good fortune for granted and value each day together. They are both warm and loving. It feels good to be in their presence.

There is only one happiness in life: to love and be loved.
George Sand

5.

Linda & Ed

WITH HER BLUE eyes and blonde hair, Linda is attractive, outspoken and smart. She speaks her mind. She is articulate and bright. She loves to travel and be active. She was married to her Irish Catholic husband for 40 years. She describes it as "they grew up together." She met him when she was 14, and they married at 17 and 18. Those were the years when they were establishing a business and raising a family. Linda's husband was 6'1" and "solid muscle."

Linda is feisty, direct and strong, as well as independent. She has the courage to make decisions others might not have made, such as moving twice as a widow. She recognizes that she is fortunate in that her resources enable her to make choices others might not be able to make—after moving the first time, when it didn't feel right, she moved again to a better place that was more suited to her liking.

She and Ed have a lot in common in that they love to travel, they both have a great attitude about enjoying life and they seem deeply appreciative of having met each other.

Linda has been a widow for almost five years and was married, with "great highs-and-lows," for 40 years.

Ed has been a widow for almost four years, and was married to his late wife, Adrienne, for 39 years. He described his marriage as "good times and bad times" because Adrienne had been "sick for a long time." He has been with Linda for "34 months and 13 days."

Linda

It was a great shock to the whole family when my husband passed away. Although my friends and family were very loving and caring, I found that I had to do a lot of comforting to others. It was a very difficult situation, my husband died very suddenly and he was very young. It was a shock to me, our son, grandchildren, and our friends. We were the youngest in our group of friends. It was shocking in so many ways and the shock just reverberated amongst our group of family and friends. In fact, a friend we had for thirty years wound up in therapy because of my husband's death.

Getting Help

I did not attend a bereavement support group right away. I went to a psychiatrist because I was having terrible trouble sleeping. The psychiatrist gave me some interim sleeping pills and advised me that it would take some time to get back into a normal pattern. He said it was very common that people have trouble sleeping after their spouses have died.

It wasn't until ten months after my husband's death that I finally joined a support group. I hopped on a cruise ship three months after my husband's death and traveled around the world by myself to get away from everyone else. I ran away for 80 days. The trip was wonderful. I was in a protective environment since my husband and I had cruised extensively. There were staff onboard ship that had known me before. Seeing me, the maitre d' said, "Oh Linda, where's Bob?" And I said, "dead." He was in shock. He asked what he could do for me and I said I would like a table of 10 and be sure to include some widows. He made it happen and I am still friendly with four of them.

I also took a cabin by myself. In case I felt like being alone, I could just go inside and slam the door. I was surprised to learn that I didn't need to do that the entire time, not *one* night.

When I returned home, I joined a bereavement support group and attended for about a year and a half. It helped to meet other people in a similar situation. We could talk together about our feelings and reactions. We got to see we were not alone and that our experiences were not that different from someone else's.

I had never lived alone before. I went right from my parent's house to marriage at age 17. The hardest thing for someone who was married young, and then married for 40 years, is learning to live alone and doing things you haven't taken care of before, for example, handling finances. I read a lot of books, including *How to Survive the Loss of a Love*. By page 20 I was determined to survive and determined to keep on reading until I read 20 to 30 bereavement books including one by Brian Weiss, who wrote about past lives.

Following the extended cruise, and 10 months of widowhood, I sold my house and moved twice. The most difficult thing was to pack up 40 years of memories, to move physically and move on emotionally. I sold the big house, I closed it up. I went through all the things that you have to do; I gave away many things.

I moved to something smaller, downsized considerably, moved to a condo, which I hated. So, I moved again within a year. I moved to a 2,000 square foot Spanish villa in a guard-gated area. It was beautiful with twenty foot ceilings and marble floors. It had been a guesthouse on property that belonged to friends of mine. It suited me and I felt very comfortable there. I lived there for a year and a half while deciding what to do with my life.

I did learn that I could live alone and be just fine. I think that was an important thing for me to do in order to move on to another relationship. I also had to know that because I might never have another relationship that I could be OK. All around me, people acknowledged what a strong woman I was, making so many major decisions by myself, but I felt I had no choice. Also, having enough money made it easier. I didn't have a lot of the problems that many widows do who are forced to downsize or alter their lifestyle by going back to work because there is no money. I was very lucky; I didn't have to do any of those things, if I choose not to. Also, having enough money makes you feel more secure so that you are not afraid to make a mistake. If you make a mistake, you can rectify it…. you are not stuck with it…like moving twice.

That first year of widowhood was very painful as one door closed and another opened. The door that closed was my life before.

Group Dating, a Start

Dating—is that more than one date? I began to date at about a year. Initially I joined a dating group—which was called 'The Gang of Six,' because we all dated each other and went out together and it was a date. It was comprised of three men and three women … informally put together.

I also went out with several men who I considered friends and decided none of them were suitable for a romantic relationship. So I sat down and considered what would I be looking for? What would I accept and what would I not accept? First of all, I wanted someone who was a widower. The main reason for that was so we could each talk about our spouses and not feel we were taking anything away from our current relationship, because what has made us the people we are today is the relationships we had in the past.

He also had to be Jewish. That might seem strange to some people because I was married to an Irish Catholic before. A lot of my friends asked, "Why would he have to be Jewish now?" I said, "Because I am tired of training." My late husband is buried in a Jewish cemetery.

By sheer coincidence, Ed's wife is buried about 40 feet from my husband. So, when we go to the cemetery, we say "hello" to both of them. And, that's also a sharing experience.

The Ready Light

When Ed and I met, I was ready for a love affair. I recognized that I was ready to sit across the table from a male at dinner and feel that wonderful male energy, something I missed. You can go out with girlfriends for dinner, but a male at a dinner table is a whole different feeling. There is a special energy that happens between a man and a woman. I wanted to feel that energy again.

But, I was also quite afraid. I was afraid of intimacy. I had known but one man in my entire life and I knew him when I was 14-years-old. Yet it was very frightening to think that I might not be able to be intimate with another male. Males have their own feelings of inadequacy but women also have them. I did feel that I was ready to begin a deep friendship, or to try to. Whether I would succeed or not, I didn't know, but I was ready.

Slow Dancing

Ed was a member of my bereavement support group. We became friends while attending the group and went to coffee every Thursday, the night the group met. Then, we also went out with our 'gang of six.'

I can now look back at my years of marriage and late spouse with clearer eyes. There were problems between us that were always a bone of contention whereas in my new relationship with Ed, they aren't there. It's a much more contented life, easier, simpler, an acceptance of who we are without trying to change each other. I think that when you become a widow and you think back over the good and bad times, you see the compromises that you made to make that marriage work. You realize that although some years were better than others, they were not all wonderful, there were some problems. You might call a truce but you might never resolve those problems.

However, when I met Ed I realized that he accepted me for exactly the way I am, that all of my 'insides' could really hang out and it was just fine. The comfort level is much higher *because* of what I lost and now have in a new life ... I am more appreciative of that life. Some of the personality traits that my late spouse didn't care for, Ed thinks are wonderful. One of the best things is being able to talk to each other about any subject and be able to tell the truth.

A Better Now

In comparing the two men, I must say that Ed is much calmer, much sweeter, and much nicer; he has already been 'seasoned.' My late husband and I grew up together. We were married at 17 and 18, unseasoned, poor, struggling. So this relationship is on an entirely different basis. It's not the mad passion of youth, but it's far more comfortable. The differences have made this new relationship smoother.

Becoming emotionally and physically intimate had its challenges though. It's very scary because you are letting yourself be open. What if it didn't work out? To be very honest, from our very first real date when we sat down and talked about ourselves and the things that we wanted, we just clicked and I remember thinking, *This is going to be permanent.* So, I was more than willing to open up my heart and not be afraid to be hurt. I'm now told every single day—twice a day actually, morning and evening—that I am loved, and what a lucky woman I am. Sometimes I feel he tells me that so I won't take him for granted—which is easy to do in a relationship. But, I do take him for granted, and that's wonderful.

Ed also made me promise I won't die before he does because he doesn't want to go through that all over again. Well, he would just have to find another woman, which he would do. He would go back to the bereavement group with his requirements, his list, and check them off.

I moved in with Ed about a year after I started dating him, but we were living together in two houses almost immediately. We didn't spend a night apart. We became close very quickly ... like a week after our first date.

Let's Get Physical

Being physically intimate again was very scary. However, I am a very physical, loving person and I have always enjoyed touching and being held except when I'm fat. And, because I had no pre-conceived notions, my performance wasn't affected at all.

I really had very few expectations. I know that might sound strange but I'd always thought that I could be sexual with another man, other than my husband, because it's fun. In fact we were able to talk about our own sexuality quite openly, quite plainly and frankly. I think at first it was a frightening experience for us to even put it into words. But, we were very open with each other. I believe it is important to consider what your partner is feeling, where they're coming from. Sexuality is the whole person—not just a penis.

Perfect? Not Quite

I will admit that there are a few problems. If anything, I find that sometimes Ed is too demanding of my time and wants me around all the time, which is a compliment but, I'm not used to being needed as much. Ed wants to get married and I don't, and I think that might be a problem. I'm trying to assess my feelings about why I don't. I just feel that it's not really important at our age. Also, I think it's a fear of being controlled and Ed can be a controlling person. All the same, I don't think there's anything that I would have done differently.

Family Trees

I was surprised that our families were so happy for the two of us. Maybe it was because they no longer had to worry about us, that Ed and I would be taking care of each other, so they wouldn't have to. I think that eventually each family realized that we were coming together as equals. My feeling is that usually, the man's family worries that the new woman might be living with him for monetary reasons, or that she would be taking their mother's things.

I made it quite clear that Number one, I had as much money as Ed and Number two, I gave all of his wife's things to his children in one fell swoop. I tease that he became very poor overnight. I believe that his wife's things belong with his children and I think they appreciated that gesture on my part.

As far as *my* family, they just wanted to make sure I was happy, that was their foremost thought. Given that, I do think it is still difficult for my son. While he hasn't said anything, nor would he, I'm sure that my son finds it difficult to see me with someone other than his father; he's an only child feeling his loss also. However, Ed, having two children of his own, promised him a sibling. Our two sons are only a year apart. It was funny how this revelation came about. Our sons and I had been standing in the entryway of Ed's house when Ed passed by, saying over his shoulder, "Oh, would you guys like a sibling?" Both of them blanched and then got red in the face. That was exactly what they *had* been picturing. I could only blurt out: "Don't even go there!"

The Road Ahead

I picture us growing older together, just having a good time, enjoying life and doing exactly as we please. Maybe I'll die on a cruise ship and we'll have a burial at sea. Then I'll have a room with a view.

My advice for others? Don't be afraid. Don't be afraid to be honest, truthful and up front. The worst thing that can happen is not being in the game, not participating in life. Many women consider that their lives are over when they become widows, that they are not going to find another person, that this is it and they are going to be 'poor me' for the rest of their lives. The truth is that if you don't get out there you won't be able to enjoy your life.

Some of the women I got to know in my bereavement support group do just that – stay closeted – and I feel sorry for them. They won't be able to enjoy their lives; they will be just waiting. My suggestion to them would be to look back, be grateful for what they had, and move on.

I even sought the advice of a psychic medium after my husband died. I asked my husband, 'Did you send me Edward?' And his answer was, 'I am sending you a short, fat Jewish man—this one's for you babe.'

Ed

My late wife's passing was a surprise. We knew she was sick and getting sicker but we didn't expect her to die—that was a surprise. From the time she went into the hospital, basically to get intravenous antibiotics, till the time she died, was ten days. Nobody thought about her actually dying until the last five-to-six days. It didn't occur to me that she was going to die.

Adrienne suffered from severe diabetes and rheumatoid arthritis with complications. She was given medication, an immune suppressant to help combat the disease and pain, and she developed a staph infection. She really couldn't fight off the infection because of her compromised immune system due to the medication.

While in the hospital, her doctor was very supportive, but there really wasn't anything anyone could do. A lot of people came to the funeral and afterward to mourn with me at home for a number of days, but the following Monday, I sent our son and daughter home and told them to go to back to work. I felt that I had the support I needed.

Outside Help

About two-and-a-half weeks after my wife's passing, I joined a bereavement support group. The group was unique in that participants were grouped according to the number of months since their spouse died. I first attended the 1 to 4-month group and didn't like that. So I moved to the second group, the 5 to 8-months of mourning and didn't like that. Finally I put myself in the 9 to 12-month group and that was where I was most comfortable and could relate to the other people.

In the first group that I joined, the other members were saying, "What am I going to do?" where the third group was already begging to think more positive, along the lines of, "What's going to happen now?" I felt more comfortable and stuck with this group. The group facilitator indicated that my healing had been rapid because Adrienne had been sick for a long time and, in a way, I was prepared for her death. I felt that it related somewhat to my experience as a businessman. I had taken some big hits in my business and had to learn to pull myself up and go on from there. So I was able to recognize that there were things that I could control and things that I couldn't.

The Verdict

The single biggest thing that helped was being with people in the same situation as myself. It became obvious very quickly that being with our old 'couple friends' was awkward for everyone. Even though I had been friendly with those people for years, it is awkward when you become single and no longer part of a couple. Within the bereavement support group, I was with a bunch of people who had lost their spouses. Also, the social contact helped because that's what I needed more than anything else.

Looking back, I'd say the hardest period for me was the day after my wife died. There was a difficult day between the day after she died and the day we put her in the ground. That was a day when decisions had to be made in terms of the funeral. But the day before the funeral was quiet. The phone didn't ring. It was the single, toughest day of all.

New Beginnings

My wife died in February and I started dating in June. A little more than three months later, I registered with the Internet matchmaking service, 'JDate.' I was ready to date because while I recognized that I had had a loss, the reality was that it was going to *stay* a loss; I didn't want to be stuck there for the rest of my life. I was lonely and I wanted to start looking for someone to share the rest of my life with.

Linda was a member of the bereavement group I attended, but I didn't meet her during the group meeting. I met her when some members of our group met for coffee afterwards. I actually met her early on, originally, but then she left the city. It wasn't until we put together our 'group of six' that I finally got to know her. I didn't think of it as dating though, it was a group of friends just going out to dinner. We became friends before we were romantically involved.

As part of this 'group of six' we not only saw each other regularly, but would call each other up and say, 'What's going on?'

At one point, a few of us, including Linda, took a long weekend trip together. When we got home, I was lonely for the first time in four days. I realized that I missed her terribly. So the next day I called her up and said, 'Would you like to have dinner?' And we went out to dinner the next night. That's when we started dating, that night. I paid for dinner, so she knew it was a date. That night we had a very scary intimate conversation and started really dating.

I talked about some personal issues that I had, things I was concerned about, and she handled the information very well. I didn't want to start a relationship with that in the background so I got it out right away. That weekend is when I considered that our relationship started.

Something New

This new relationship hasn't changed my feeling for my late wife. Not at all. My late spouse was my life before, and she passed away through no fault of mine, no fault of hers. It's just a fact of life and I'm going on.

Linda and I have an entirely different relationship than the relationship I had with my late wife. With Linda, the two biggest problem-areas between a man and a woman, money and children, are mute. We have only one purpose in our relationship and that is to laugh and have fun. We are very rigid about pursuing that goal.

Cards on the Table

It was scary to become emotionally vulnerable again. The first night when we sat down and had an intimate conversation it was terrifying, but once we got past that, it was terrific. I don't know what today's expectations of sexuality are, or that it has any bearing. We needed to become intimate so that we could go on from there. We had to get over this challenge so that we could then explore all these other areas. It helped that we had become friends in those prior three months in which we didn't have those expectations.

Pushing the Envelope

My expectations went beyond the hope of holding hands and kissing. I'm a touchy-feely kind of guy. I needed somebody to touch and feel. I guess I kind of backed Linda up against that wall. Nonetheless, it wasn't easy.

It was terrifying, not comfortable. Once we talked about it, from then on, it's been comfortable.

To Have and Have Knots

Sure, problems arose, particularly on two occasions. The first one was when we were on our first cruise together. She wanted to buy a scarf. "Should I get this?" she asked. I answered, "Do you need it?" Well, she did not like *that* answer. Let's just say that it caused an important discussion about communication.

On another occasion, she told me she didn't like the way my clothes were hung in the closet—falling off hangers. I said, 'I'm taking my book and I'll see you in a couple of hours. I don't like the way you are talking to me.' It was her tone of voice when she criticized me for my sloppy ways. Linda stomped on my clothes and then hung them up. We met for lunch and worked it out.

In retrospect, though, there's nothing I would have done very differently.

Periods of Adjustment

In our bereavement support groups, Linda and I had seen some participants having problems with family members' acceptance of a new relationship. So, we tried to be very careful. We tried to make sure that our kids were not offended by avoiding what others had done to offend their adult kids. We were aware that there were dangers and tried to conduct ourselves so nothing did occur.

What the future holds is this, Party – party – party. Linda and I like to laugh a lot together.

My advice to others? Recognize that you have had a loss, accept it and get past it. Think about what you want to do and how you want to spend the rest of your life. Go out and find whatever way works. Plan your work and work your plan. Find activities that interest you.

Reflections

Ed has a wonderful attitude about life. Ed says, "We are not going to change each other. We allow each other to get angry because it's over very quickly." His late wife was sweeter and more manipulative, while Linda is outspoken and doesn't manipulate. She is direct in her approach. Pressures and stress don't build with this couple. Ed likes the fact that Linda is a strong woman. She and Ed have a lot in common in that they love to travel, they both have a great attitude about enjoying life and they seem deeply appreciative of having met each other to enjoy life with.

You come to love not by finding the perfect person,
but by seeing an imperfect person perfectly.
Sam Keen

6.

Sydel & Jerry

SYDEL IS AN ATTRACTIVE blonde and Jerry a cute guy with an easy grin. They like to share stories about what has happened to them. Jerry had been married for 34 years and Sydel for 45 years. She was 18 when she married and Jerry was 30. They seem very supportive of each other, and at the same time very different. Jerry had a very hard time in his early bereavement because he was so angry.

Sydel has been a widow for five years. Jerry has been a widower for five.

Sydel

After my husband passed away, my son flew down to Southern California from Reno once a month to be with me. My daughters were always around, always available by telephone. My husband's sister was also a great help; she was always around or she'd call and say, "I'm going to the movies and you're coming too." Several friends were also available and helpful to me.

About three months after my husband died, I joined a bereavement support group, and attended for two years. I had found that family and friends couldn't quite relate to my feelings. None of them had gone through losing a spouse. Within my support group, I was with people who knew how I felt and didn't mind if I cried when I tried to speak, and I didn't mind either. I also made my own friends in the group. After leaving the formal support group, a few friends from there still meet once a week for dinner, and once a month with the larger, post-support group for dinner.

The Elephant in the Room

The first two or three months were the hardest. I missed my husband. He was also my law partner, so I also had to adjust to running the practice myself. And I was scared … about a lot of things. That was not a good time. After about three months, an acquaintance that I didn't even know very well called several times, encouraging me to attend a bereavement support group. My answer to her was, "Why? I'm doing fine." To which she answered, "You are not doing fine." So I went.

It's a Date

About two years after my husband died, I began dating. I always knew that I was going to try to find another partner. Two years just seemed to be the right time and I had an opportunity. Jerry came into our bereavement support group for the first time and, as it happened, it was the day the facilitator gave out rosters. He called me the next day and said, "I didn't like the group but I would like to see you." I felt I was ready to start a deep friendship although I had already been dating other men, in fact, one seriously.

At first I dated Jerry just as a friend ... or so I told myself. He is nothing like my late husband. It's like apples and oranges. Jerry is very different from Sheldon and everyone else in the whole world.

My late husband was a very restful person; he was easy to be around. He was very calm most of the time; he didn't get upset easily. He was extremely efficient. But he could also be very remote and aloof. His favorite pastime was watching television. He wasn't helpful around the house, except for making repairs; he was very good at that.

Jerry, in contrast, worries a lot, thinks that he knows everything and what's right for everyone else. I have to remind him not to nag. He's very helpful; whatever he's doing, he does without even asking and he's much more demonstrative than Sheldon. More hugs and kisses, and he's a lot of fun. He likes to watch television, but he also likes to do things. I've tried new things with him, like cruising, that I had never done before. And he is learning to play bridge, which I enjoy.

Closer and Closer

Before meeting Jerry, I had already enjoyed another intimate relationship, so I knew it wouldn't be a problem. With the first relationship, I was terrified for about five minutes. I didn't know if I could respond physically to anyone beside my late husband. Getting emotionally involved with Jerry was not scary, we were already friends and I knew him pretty well. I liked the fact that he seemed to be completely honest—sometimes too honest.

I had never dated before I married my husband; I was 15 when I met him. My parents hated him and the situation. He wasn't a doctor, lawyer, accountant or dentist and his parents were European, rather than American born. And they didn't have much money. My parents didn't realize that I was very shy, didn't have many friends, and that I wouldn't have had that much to offer. I was not in a profession at that time and had very little self confidence. Boy, have I changed! In regard to sexuality, my shyness didn't seem to affect my performance … in fact, I learned some very nice things! I had always enjoyed sex and was not ready to give it up. I can talk to Jerry about sex – or about anything. It may start an argument but that's OK too.

One of the things I needed to talk about was my former relationship – to tell Jerry it had broken up and the reason why. I had discovered that he'd been sleeping with other women. I had to take an AIDS test, which sort of cramped our sex life for awhile. Jerry knew the other man, which was uncomfortable.

Do-Overs?

I can't think of anything I would have done differently because I really liked that other relationship while it lasted. I don't like the way it ended. But with Jerry, everything isn't always smooth either, especially where family is concerned.

Jerry tends to pontificate, to nag and belabor his point, and my younger daughter and grandchildren think he talks down to them. They really don't like him that much- especially my 10-year-old grandson.

Regardless, I have made a commitment to him and I expect it to last – till death do us part, but whether we'll get married or not, I don't know. That could create problems. I don't feel the need to remarry – although Jerry would like it. There are financial problems; we have a huge disparity in finances; they might iron out sometime later, but I'm not in a hurry.

Advice to others? I would recommend that people try to meet someone and if and when they do, *go for it*. So many people say that they don't want another relationship because it, too, could end in death, which I can appreciate, but if you don't take risks, you don't get rewards or enjoyment.

Jerry

After my wife's death, my main support was from my sons, especially the one I work with full time and am closer to because of that. For about six weeks after my wife's passing, I received lay-counseling and support from a bereavement volunteer from my synagogue. About a month later, I joined a bereavement support group that met once a week. When I joined the group, I was the only man. Unfortunately this group wasn't able to sustain, but I was able to talk to the facilitator by phone for support and help. This facilitator knew of another bereavement support group that met weekly and suggested I check it out. I did, and stayed with this group for over two years.

I Understand

I came to an important, helpful understanding of what the loss of a spouse is all about, something I hadn't really been able to comprehend. My mother lost my father when she was about the same age as I when I lost my late wife. I finally knew after it happened to me, how little I understood what this might have meant to my mother. I was always there for my mother but I didn't comprehend what it was all about. I knew about losing an uncle or a grandfather but I did not comprehend what it was like losing a spouse when my father died.

After losing my wife, and until I joined this bereavement support group, yes, I was breathing, but I didn't understand myself and what I was feeling. I didn't understand my new position in the world or my new relationship to other people very well. Just because I'm a creature of habit and worked regularly all my life, I tried to maintain some of those functions, working and being there with my son, but I was just going through the motions ... habit.

Intellectually, I knew what I was supposed to be doing each day. Get out of bed. Just try to function, cut the lawn, clean the swimming pool, do things … but there wasn't any emotional understanding of what was going on in my life. I didn't have any emotional connection.

Burning Anger

After the first two months of being widowed, the most difficult part was that I didn't fully understand *why* she died. It was very sudden. A doctor, not my late wife's attending physician, but a business friend of mine, told me after hearing the circumstance of my wife's death, that he felt my wife did not die of natural causes, but of medical malpractice. I went ballistic. I was outraged. I could think of nothing—morning, noon and night—except revenge and punishment towards the medical people I felt killed my wife.

Finally my family doctor suggested a medication, an antidepressant, to help relieve some of the anxiety and anger. It did help, I felt calmer. Between the medication and my bereavement support group I was able to get through that first year. During this year, the group facilitator also suggested that I seek psychiatric help to deal with my anger. Their fear was that I might act on this anger.

I prayed almost every day that I would not act on my anger. I have two children and I thought their lives would be better if I were alive. Doing myself in, or doing someone else in and winding up in jail for the rest of my life, were not good options. I wanted to be there for my children. I knew I was a good person and that the world would not be a better place without me.

So, I started to write poetry in my support group to help others in the group and didn't understand at all that I was also helping myself, that it was a form of therapy. I came to realize that later, much later. At a conscious level I was motivated to write because I wanted to help others.

After a couple of months in the support group I felt that I was in better shape, better able to care for myself and maybe glimpse a better future. I continued on the medication during the second year although in some ways I felt like a walking zombie. I had less feeling emotionally than I thought was normal. I am not an addictive type of person. Anything that seems to control me is something that I fight. I never was addicted to cigarettes, drugs, coffee or anything. I don't like the fact that the medication was controlling my moods, keeping me on this even keel, when I wasn't necessarily an even-keeled person. I didn't want to be out of control, but I didn't want to be a zombie either.

My doctor slowly reduced my dosage, and then switched my medication to another antidepressant, one which made me feel more myself. I finally felt like a 'real' person again. It was at that point that I felt comfortable dating again.

Testing the Waters

During the end of the first year of grieving and after switching medications, I began to go out a little bit. I would join others from my support group in social events, or would take someone to lunch or dinner. That was about it. By the next year, I started to go out a little bit more.

During my second year of grieving, I began dating Sydel. At first it was nothing romantic, just a friendship thing. Maybe once a month we would go to a movie or dinner. There was no heavy romantic involvement at that time. Then I went to a few parties for single adults, met a few women and went on a couple of dates. I began to get the idea that I was something of a man in demand.

Perhaps unlike most people, I have always felt comfortable being alone. I never felt overwhelmed with a need for intimacy - that's at a conscious level. Perhaps at an unconscious level, my needs might have been much different. To me, I was just a strong person but I also knew that I would never be happy or satisfied with my life without a committed relationship with a woman. I didn't get married till I was thirty years old so I had a good long period of time where I was a single guy. But I wasn't satisfied with that existence. I am not a happy-go-lucky, single bar-hopping man. So I knew I had to be connected and I needed to make an effort to try to find that connection.

Memories Die Hard

Sydel and I became friends before becoming more deeply involved, but I see no link between what's happening in my life now, and the relationship I had with my late wife.

There's nothing now that's relevant to my relationship with my late wife. That was a life I had, and when she died that life was ended, and part of my life ended. It was a lot of pain and emotional suffering. So in a sense, that has no influence or direct connection to my present life.

I still suffer in a number of ways but I would be suffering whether I was connected to Sydel or not. I'm still going to a psychologist for private sessions, although instead of once a week I now go once a month. I'm not sure the psychologist is helping all that much and maybe I should make a change. It might be good to talk to somebody else but my psychologist is male and I don't have any intelligent, certainly psychologically educated male friends that I could to talk to, so it's probably not a bad idea to be doing this.

I never had male friends, probably never will, just not my thing. It's still difficult, almost five years later, for me to look at my late wife's picture or talk about her without breaking down and crying from the sheer sadness of the loss, not just my loss but how tragically and unexpectedly she had life taken away from her. That's the real hard part. If she had been hit by a bus, somehow the brakes failed, that would have been 'life in the big city and tough luck,' but not at the hands of doctors who were supposed to keep her alive, who did what they could to kill her, though they didn't plan it that way.

A New Outlook

Sydel is very different. It is important to know that once we became a committed, loving couple, for about two and a half years now, I have felt true happiness. During the first half of my bereavement there was virtually no happiness, and in the second half, there has been happiness most of the time. I don't suppose there is happiness all of the time.

No two people are alike. My wife and I had a good marriage; we had very few significant disagreements. My wife was previously married; she married her high school sweetheart. The marriage ended while she was pregnant with their first child, so her son grew up in a household with his mother and grandmother with no strong male connection for five years. When we married, and with the biological father's consent, I adopted him.

Sydel has a different personality, a different way of expressing herself, a different intellect from my late wife. She communicates her thoughts and feelings immediately and with more authority than my wife did. My late wife was more into herself; she didn't share her thoughts as readily.

In the Bedroom

Sydel is an understanding and caring person, we both wanted to become intimate *and* protective of each other.

We have always been concerned with each other's feelings and well-being. We are intelligent and mature, and that, I believe, has been the cornerstone of our relationship.

We have our own, independent values and thoughts and are not influenced by popular culture regarding sexual expectations or other issues. Mutual satisfaction is our goal. We didn't verbally discuss intimacy a whole lot. Sometimes you just do what comes naturally.

Money, however, was a question. I suppose financial concerns are always some kind of a question. It is more my concern than Sydel's. I've got children, she's got children. None of the children have significantly interfered in our relationship, but there's never been the need. For the most part, they all seem pretty happy that we have each other and that we are not alone. If they had any misgivings, we would not like it, but I don't think it would have any significant bearing on anything.

The future looks promising. I wouldn't have done anything any differently. My family likes Sydel and they get along well. And my hope is that our relationship will continue to grow and become permanent. My advice? Pursue happiness by developing a new, committed, loving relationship because I believe that is the natural order of things.

Jerry and Sydel seem very supportive of each other, and at the same time very different. Jerry had a very hard time in his early bereavement because he was so angry. His anger was accessible to him, and it provided a particularly touching glimpse of his growth and changes over time. He is a very sensitive man, as shown by his poetry. The fact that he began to see how his creative energy helped him to heal his anger is wonderful.

Here are two people that wanted to make a connection and worked hard at it. They both have a sense of humor and an ability to laugh at themselves. They come from very different backgrounds. Sydel seems very appreciative of Jerry's warmth, caring and willingness to pitch in and help. He seems much less formal than her husband was. They both say that the relationship they have now is different from the one they had before.

It is particularly nice to hear that they are learning new skills together and separately, engaging in life and enjoying it. Sydel recently retired and Jerry is still working. They display a genuine fondness for each other, are glad they have found each other as partners, and are making a good adjustment by moving from sadness to the pleasure of life again.

Love does not consist in gazing at each other
but in looking together in the same direction.
Antoine de Saint-Exupery

The Newlyweds
An improbable love story
Martha Weinman Lear

LATELY WE'VE BEEN bringing joy to total strangers.

How? Easy. We got married.

It began like this; One icy day last winter, we headed down to the bureau of licenses in lower Manhattan. There was a security guard at the door, a big, beefy fellow, and Albert asked him where to go for a license.

"What kind of license?" the guard said.

"Marriage," Albert said.

Marriage! The guard stared at our faces, which clearly belonged (still do) to a pair of septuagenarians. And then the guard went totally gaga:

"You folks are getting married? Fan-tastic!" Pulled off his cap and waved it in the frigid air. Took off a glove, grabbed Albert's hand in his massive paw.

"You've made my day! Hey, Mike, come over here. Get this! These folks are getting married!" Mike also went gaga.

We went to buy a wedding band. The saleswoman looked at Albert, looked at me and looked uncertain. "For ... your daughter?" she asked cautiously.

"For us," Albert said.

"For *you*? Oooh-ooh! I just *love* it. Helen! Stacy! Listen!" Helen, who was maybe 40, and Stacy, who looked like a high-schooler, loved it too.

It kept happening. The florist, the wine merchant, the cake-maker for our small family wedding ... strangers all. At first we couldn't figure it out. Why were people going bananas about the marriage of a pair of total strangers?

Soon after the ceremony, we went to a party where we were introduced to a woman as newlyweds, and she said, "Oh, my goodness!" Hands clasped to bosom, dreamy smile. "You've made me so *happy*, I could cry." And, in fact, her eyes brimmed over.

Now we got it. How could we not? It had nothing to do with us, really (oh, sure, with the way we looked; but beyond that, nothing). It was all about themselves. Somehow, this marriage made them feel good about themselves—about their own hopes that might not have been fulfilled, and which they thought might never be fulfilled. Especially in the department of love.

I checked out our theory with our longtime friend, Dr. Ethel Person, the noted Manhattan psychiatrist and psychoanalyst. "Oh," she said. "You're *exactly* right. *Exactly*. There is such a powerful bias in this country toward believing that over a certain age, unless you're with someone, you'll never be with anyone again. For people to see a pair like you, opens up new possibilities for themselves. You become a wordless message that there can be new beginnings, second chances all through the life cycle."

But it is not just about love. We are also talking about work, friends, family connections, new ambitions, new adventures—as Dr. Person says, "renewal in every way."

It is sweet stuff, renewal—especially when unexpected. And I certainly did not expect it.

I had been widowed for many years when Albert came along. There had been other men in those years. Fine men, worthy of loving, but never, as it happened, any I did love or wanted to share the rest of my life with. Which was okay. I had those pleasant romances, I had my work, my cherished friends, and I could have gone on like that and been just fine. But face it: Love is more. Love is bigger. Love is other.

Then I went one evening to the home of friends for dinner. Table set for six (my favorite dinner-party number, the coziest, absolutely the best for conversation), and the sixth was the proverbial tall, handsome stranger—lanky, cute gray Van-dyke beard, somewhat austere.

It was not a fix-up. He was a recent widower, "a basket case," my hosts told me sotto voce. They hoped to draw him out.

At the table, someone asked how long ago his wife had died. Eight months, he said. And suddenly, with no warning whatsoever, I found myself catapulted back through time to when I had been just eight months widowed, to precisely how that had felt, and I lost it. I began to cry, not decorously but loudly, pungently, the for-heaven's-sake-go-blow-your-nose kind of crying, and I mumbled my apologies and ran to another room.

He followed me. It stunned me then, and stuns me still—this man who bore such grief of his own should come to comfort *me*. He was no longer austere. He sat down beside me, gave me his handkerchief, peered into my face and said, "I know, I know."

It made a powerful, instant connection. It enabled us to bypass the usual getting-to-know-you stuff, because people who've had the experience of losing a beloved one already *do* know one another in a special, intimate way—a way those who've never mourned really can't understand.

He called the next week to invite me to dinner. It was an awkward call. ("Remember," he said later, "I hadn't asked a woman for a date in 40 years. What if you'd said no?" As for myself, all through that long week I had been thinking: Damn it, why doesn't he call? Doesn't he want that handkerchief back?) But from the first evening together, it was a total comfort zone.

We became An Item, which seemed to please our families and friends. ("My grandpa has a girlfriend," his six-year-old granddaughter told her neighbors.) After a year—ah, impetuous youth!—we combined households. My closest friends gave a party for us, in the apartment I was leaving. Swell party, warm toasts. But it was this past winter, when we decided to marry—well, that's when everyone got *really* twinkly. Including the butcher, the baker, and the candlestick-maker. Everyone.

I have been thinking about this a lot. We all love love, of course. But I suspect that what everyone loves even more is second-time-around love. It seems to speak to each observer in a more personal way. I look into the pleasure-glazed eyes of strangers and I think, this makes you feel good, does it? Terrific. Be my guest.

Life without love is like a tree without blossoms or fruit.
by Kahlil Gibran, The Vision"

7.

Helen & Jack

IF THERE ARE TWO MORE forward-looking, vital, positive thinking 80-something people on this planet, they have yet to be identified. Helen and Jack, gracious and warm as individuals and as a couple, are committed to enjoying life and each other, moment-by-moment. Together they live in Helen's lovely Hollywood hills home decorated with memorabilia of their current travels around the globe and past travels with their late spouses.

Helen and Jack beautifully exemplify the reality that it gets easier when "seniors" get together to form a new relationship ... no kids, and rarely money problems, to argue over.

Helen was married for almost 53 years; she has been a widow for eight. Jack was married for 57 years; a widow for several years

Helen

After my husband died, friends and family rallied 'round. My friends were wonderful. My kids were good, but they don't live here, in Los Angeles, and that's a significant factor. We talked on the phone and they came to visit, but they just weren't able to be here on a daily basis. I did, however, use my daughter as a long-distance crutch; I would call her every morning.

I was very fortunate because I not only had wonderful friends, but I had a neighbor, Marjie, who is a blessing for anyone to know. Other people questioned why I would want to continue to live in my house all alone. It's in the Hollywood Hills area and not very accessible. Marjie never questioned my decision to stay put, but rather was a constant source of support whenever I needed any kind of help. I have always lived my life running *to*, not *from* challenges. Certainly I could have moved up to Northern California to live near my daughter. Even though at that point I didn't know what I wanted to do, I did know that I wanted to stay in my home. My answer at that time was to continue my familiar activities, including travel.

The First Step

I had a friend who insisted that I come to her support group. So I attended twice. It didn't click for me. I didn't want to listen to other people's sad stories. I realized that I was more fortunate than most others. My late husband had always said, "You can get along without me, but I can't get along without you." There was a reason for his feeling this way. When he turned 70 he was thrilled because his father and brother had both died much younger. He never expected to make it to 70 and was in shock when he did. And so, the reality is that I just knew that my life expectancy would be greater than his.

A Different Role

While I hadn't taken care of the family finances before, I knew how to, or asked for help when I needed it. I had to meet with lawyers, but it wasn't a big deal. I knew that there were a lot of things that I had to do and just dug in … I became very well acquainted with the people who ran the bank.

The kind of challenges I had seem trivial now, but were major obstacles during those first few months of mourning. But a close, dear cousin who lives on the east coast said, when we knew that my husband was dying, 'I won't come for the funeral, but I will come afterward, when you need me.' It was a wonderful thing to say and so wonderful for me to have her come. In the first place, she came just as my children were leaving, so I didn't have time to feel, 'Oh, I'm all alone.'

There were so many things that she helped me with during the 10 days that she spent with me. I was so very, very tired during that time and when I commented to her that I didn't understand why, she offered comfort with the words, 'That's what happens when you're grieving because it's an emotional strain.'

Then the sink got plugged up. Now I laugh, but that was something that had never been a problem for me; I always had someone who took care of it. And I got through that one. It was a real help to me to know that I could survive this thing. It's funny now, but at the time it was overwhelming.

Up and Out

Before meeting Jack I would go out and socialize with groups of friends, but no "dating." I belong to a lot of organizations and continued to be very active. I met Jack through a mutual friend; I'll let Jack tell you about our getting together.

Our relationship from the very beginning has been very, very comfortable. We have so many things in common even though we hadn't known each other before. As an example, on our first date I discovered that years before he had attended the same Boston school as did my late husband. We just clicked right away. My philosophy is that I live in the moment. And Jack and I both feel that this is the life we have to live. You cannot live in the past. That was then and this is now.

A Brave New World

Becoming emotionally vulnerable again was not hard for me at all. We're not 15-years-old and we don't fall in love the same way we might have then. Also, we each maintain a certain amount of independence and I think that's important. It's easy. As long as we have our health, it's good.

Exploring physical intimacy came naturally too. It's comfortable, and that describes *everything* about our relationship. If there had been any concerns, we would have been very comfortable voicing them, but we didn't really have any. I wouldn't have done anything differently, absolutely nothing.

A Family Votes

My children and particularly my son, were very accepting of my relationship with Jack. It was a burden off their shoulders. When each met the other's adult children, it was just so easy. Kids, regardless of their age, are happy when their parents are happy.

By example, my Dad had taught me to be very self-sufficient. Of course I wouldn't wish it on anyone else to learn self-sufficiency that way, but I knew even as a child that I was fortunate. My mother died when I was 6-years-old. And I was very fortunate to have such a wonderful father. He was father, mother, sister and brother to me. I would sometimes suggest he think about remarriage and he said 'No,' he was not going to bring a stepmother into the house.

Consequently, I was able to do a lot of adult things at an early age because he would take me to adult functions and I enjoyed it. I didn't mind being the only youngster there … it made me feel special. In keeping with the saying, 'If you get lemons, make lemonade,' that's the way he did it. When I married and moved to California from Boston, he came out about three months later to visit. My husband and I had already decided that we would build a house here and that we would build a room for him so that he would have privacy. After getting his affairs in order, a year later he moved here permanently. To keep himself busy, he decided to take a real estate class as it was a booming business at that time. As chance would have it an old acquaintance was also in that class. One thing led to another and they married. He was also a wonderful example that life goes on. They were married for 27 years and traveled all over the world together.

Love, Not Marriage

Jack and I plan to spend the rest of our lives living together. We feel that marriage is not necessary. I consider myself fortunate in that I have always believed that I have a guardian angel watching over me ... someone to help me. My advice? Look forward, not backward.

Jack

After my wife died, I coped by keeping busy with club activities and friends. One close friend was David, whom I had known for many, many years. Not only were we classmates together at the Boston Latin School, but after losing track of one another after graduation, we had rediscovered each other again as adults and resumed a close friendship. After years of going our separate ways after college, I called him, and as soon as he heard my voice on the phone he said, "Jack, how the hell are you?" It was just amazing.

David and his wife, Dodie, became close friends with my wife and me. But here's the really funny part. It turns out that Helen and Dodie had been classmates at Wellesley years before in Boston and had remained friends all these years. Helen and her late husband were friends with David and Dodie, as were my wife and I. So as it happened, Helen and I had had mutual friends for a long time. Strangely, it turned out that, whenever my wife and I had social functions or got together with David and Dodie, Helen and her husband were not present and visa-versa, so my wife and I never met Helen or her husband.

I continued to get together with Dodie and David after my wife died, and after about a year had passed, Dodie called to say, "Look, I want to do something." And I said, "What?" "I'm going to give you the name of three women who were classmates of mine at Wellesley." Three of them happened to be living in the LA area. "I'll give you their phone numbers and whatever you want to do with the numbers is okay with me."

I wrote the names and numbers down. One I discarded right away because she was a divorcee and traveling all over the world. I called the third name, took her to lunch and that was the end of that. Helen was number two on the list. I decided to call Helen, but I would start to dial and hang up, start to dial and hang up again, until finally I had the courage to complete the call.

Helen answered and I said "Hi, my name is Jack'." Helen responded with, "Well, how can I help you?" Helen thought I was trying to sell her something so I quickly added, "I think we have a mutual friend, Dodie, and that it is my understanding that you and Dodie were classmates at Wellesley, and that David and I were classmates at Boston Latin, and I'm not trying to sell you anything."

I finally got up my courage and said, "I haven't asked anybody for a date in 60 years ... would you have lunch with me one day?" So we went to lunch and the rest is history. Now, when I say the rest is history, I mean we clicked together, we decided we were meant to be with each other.

The Basics

We had similar backgrounds, we came from the same area, Boston; we had close mutual friends. We had a level of comfort right away. I would hope that everyone could find the kind of relationship that we have.

We didn't decide to live together on the spur of the moment. It took about four months before we decided, when we saw that this relationship was getting better all the time. Before moving in together, I'd spend weekends at Helen's house. On Sunday night I'd tell her that I had to go home tonight because my cleaning lady is coming in the morning.

We told people about our plan to live together at some informal get-together with friends. Neighbors, such as Marjie's husband, John, said it was no surprise to him as he'd been seeing my car parked in Helen's driveway over the weekends and assumed a new relationship was the cause.

We told people that we would not be married, but it was important too that they knew I would be giving Helen a sum of money every year to cover 50 percent of our living expenses. It was also important to let them and our families know that any assets we had before coming together would remain separate. That is, what was mine would remain mine and visa-versa.

No Big Thing

Becoming intimate was relatively easy. It was so comfortable. My philosophy is that, whatever is going to happen is going to happen. We can't predict what will happen tomorrow. But if I should pass away, that's it; it was good enough. We live in the moment. In a couple of months I'm going to be 85 years old, I don't think that I'm on borrowed time, but how much longer will I be around? Who knows? Helen will be 82 in another month, so we have to enjoy life while we can, that's my feeling. To make the most of what we can out of the life that we have left and have some fun.

Don't Look Back

I don't look back because after all, my first marriage was my only marriage and it was good ...the children were born and then the grandchildren. My wife had been ill for seven years and she was in the hospital for about seven weeks before she died. I have never found myself comparing Helen with my late wife. And our families have been supportive.

Helen and I traveled to Washington D.C. to meet her son. When he drove us to the airport to return home to California, he made a remark that I will never forget. As we were saying our goodbyes, he gave me a big hug and said, "I want to thank you, Jack, for being responsible for making my mother laugh for the first time (since losing my father)." And my kids met Helen and everyone just jelled, it just locked in.

We're going to be a couple that wants to spend the rest of our years together, but we've decided that we are not going to be formally married. While what I have materially is of far less value than what she has, still it's something that's mine, and I don't want our respective families to think that I am going to take anything that is rightfully theirs. We've been together a little over four years now and it has been great with both families.

I gave up my apartment and moved into Helen's home. I gave up a lot of my stuff, the valuables went to the kids; I brought some furniture and things with me. Friends say you'd never know that we were blending two house holds; everything looks as if it belongs. And we're very comfortable. My kids are happy that we have a great relationship and that they don't have to call every day to see how good ol' dad is getting along. They know I'm getting along fine.

Around the Corner

With our respective ages and backgrounds, we decided not to be married. Between us we have had 110 years of very successful first marriages, 57 for me, and 53 for her. We talked to her local clergyman to tell him what we had in mind. He thought it was not a bad idea but suggested that we have an informal agreement drawn up and we did. Not in the form of any pre-nuptial agreement, but I would not want to be a gigolo.

Here's my tip for others: Get comfortable as soon as possible. I have an expression I heard long ago that I believe applies, "It's not a good idea to get old, just get *older.*"

Reflections

I loved when Helen commented, "I have always lived my life running to, not from, challenges." I get the impression of energy and love of life and delight in being actively engaged in living. Refreshing! Helen seems to have an "up" and "open" attitude. She seems to flow with what she has to learn in life and move forward from that place. The new learning presents itself as exciting rather than depleting. I get the feeling of energy and a wonderful spirit. Helen has respect for the philosophical approach of "living in the moment," when she exclaimed that: "Jack and I both feel that this is the life we have to live. You cannot live in the past. That was then and this is now."

The recognition that they are not 15-year olds who had fallen in love as only 15-year-olds can is a healthy attitude. You might feel 15, but you know more. Adolescent feelings may come along with new dating, but people also bring their experiences with them.

Helen acknowledges that "My children were very accepting of my relationship with Jack. It was a burden off their shoulders." Grown children may feel really good when they see their parent happy, less lonely and sharing companionship. It also lightens the burden they may feel in regard to responsibility. Helen's dad had taught her to be very self-sufficient. This served her well when she was widowed.

Helen was widowed for eight years and Jack for several years, when they met. They had similar backgrounds, came from the same area in Boston and had close mutual friends. Once they met, they felt that they were meant to be with each other. They shared a degree of comfort right away. Jack's philosophy is that, "Whatever is going to happen is going to happen. We can't predict what will happen tomorrow. But, if I should pass away, it was good enough." Living in the moment seems to be important to both of them. They share a great attitude about enjoying life while they can, making the most of what they have out of life, and having fun.

It was touching when Helen's son thanked Jack for helping his mother to laugh again. This is a couple that wants to spend the rest of their lives together.

What many re-connected couples seem to have in common is a joy of each other, an appreciation of each other and a gratitude that they have met. They are aware that problems raising kids are gone and financial tensions of early years are not predominant. What is predominant now is caring for and loving each other in the moment, and enjoying it for as long as it will last.

In dreams and in love there are no impossibilities.
Janos Arany

8.

Frank & Michael

SOMETIMES LIFE DOESN'T fit into a neat pattern of losing
a loved one, and then, moving on to a new, loving and
committed relationship. As in the case of Frank and
Michael, Frank met Michael two years before his previous
partner passed away, in fact, Frank and Tim had already
gone their separate ways. However, regardless of the time
span, Frank was impacted by his former partner's death in
a way that would surprise him. It would unfold in his
questioning the relationship with Tim and his death, and
what it meant to his relationship with Michael. There is
great value in revisiting important times of our lives that
we might simply have blocked out emotionally because
they were too painful to process at the time.

Frank has worked in the Mental Health field since
1985. Presently he is the intake and assessment clinician
for Children's Advocacy Center in Florida where they deal
primarily with victims of abuse—physical, sexual and
emotional—and provide group, individual and family

therapy. He also runs a therapy group for parents of children (6-9) who have been sexually abused.

Michael works at Kmart and is the receiving manager. He has been with them for 13 years and is looking forward to the changes that will come about as a result of it becoming a Sears' Essentials store in the near future. He's on a Monday – Friday work schedule, as is Frank, so they have weekends to enjoy each other and their friends. How does Michael describe Frank? "That's easy," says Michael, "Frank just lights up a room when he walks into it."

Frank

Tim and I met in NYC in July, 1981, and we were together until 1992. Tim passed away two years later in 1994. After Tim's death, I received a tremendous amount of support from friends who had known the two of us. When we split, we were living in Rochester, N.Y.; I had gone back to NYC and then on to Florida so there was no "community" support available, but I am sure I could have accessed Hospice had I felt that I needed it at the time.

Out of the Blue

I was able to relive the good times in my head—it was funny how things that had nothing to do with Tim and I as a couple, could trigger a memory of him. I also slipped a few times and referred to Michael (my present partner of four years) as Tim—which did not go over too well.

The hardest time was the initial period, Tim died in a tragic manner. He was flying home from London and went into a diabetic coma; the plane emergency-landed in Dublin where he died of a heart attack. He was alone with no family or friends with him; that bothered me the most.

The Wheel Turns

I met Michael at a local bar. I was living on the East Coast of Florida and had business on the West Coast of Florida. After we met, Michael commuted back and forth, traveling from one side of the state to the other, a three hour drive by car so that we could be together. At that time, I was also a caregiver for my mother. When she passed away I stayed where I was and we continued to commute for six months until I realized that gas 'wasn't getting any cheaper' and I relocated permanently. But I'm getting ahead of myself.

We met in April 2001 while I was in Fort Myers on business. If there is such a thing as love at first sight, this was it. After the fourth weekend, Michael began making that three-hour drive on weekends until Sept. 2001 when I sold my house and moved in with my ailing mother. I was also a foster parent at the time and it was much easier for Michael to drive over than for me to find the child/parent care I would have needed to be able to make the drive to him.

My mother passed away in September, '02 from colon cancer and I stayed in the house, again commuting on weekends. In February, I said, 'This is ridiculous; we could and should be living together.' I put some money down on a new house in Cape Coral, found a job in mental health in Fort Myers and moved in with Michael in May, 2003 in his apartment. Our house was ready in April of the next year.

We are your typical married couple sharing the duties of running a house while both are working full time. As we live 10 miles outside of any civilization and neither of us is disciplined enough to be the designated driver, we stay home and entertain ourselves and have a very limited social network here in Fort Myers. We do go away a lot and fly to NYC at least four or five times a year for long weekends. That seems to satisfy my cultural needs as we usually book tickets for a play or musical while there.

First, the Physical

Michael and I started off right from the git-go; we knew that this was IT. As with most (if not all) of my relationships in the past, ours started out as a highly charged sexual one. Over four years it has grown into a true partnership where spooning at night is just as important as the physical act of making love. He is a part of life in every way; family, social and work. I have watched him grow in very positive ways, and would like to think I had some influence in that growth.

By way of an example, his father developed Alzheimer's and had to be placed in a nursing home. To his credit, Michael was able to navigate that incredibly difficult road of applying for state aid ... all without leaving bodies of civil service workers in his wake.

His mother passed away just after Easter and he was able to help her meet this last challenge in life in a very peaceful manner while also honoring her wishes to the end. (No Terri Schiavo case here.) His life challenges have been met head-on and he has grown as a son, man, lover and partner; I am truly fortunate to have met him.

The Journey
Tim and I did not end on a very amicable note; I think we both would have run each over with a car if we knew we could get away with it. It took a good ten years before I could think of him without getting hot under the collar. Meeting Michael helped end much of the animosity I felt. I finally realized life was too short to harbor those feelings. I wish I could have realized that sooner.

With Tim, the focus was always on him; he was a ballet dancer/instructor/creative director who just loved being in the spotlight. I was the one licking envelopes for fundraisers, cleaning the studio after everyone left, and the house. Resentment, you bet! With Michael it is a true partnership; he was so helpful to me when my mother passed away and I like to think I was there for him when his mom recently passed away.

High Hopes
My expectations for sexual and emotional intimacy were for a hell of a lot more than I had with Tim. Michael and I are very open with what we need, want and desire.

Overall, this is probably the smoothest path to love that I've ever ventured down.

With Michael I would not do anything differently. When Tim passed away, it did force me to reconnect with some old feelings and, thankfully, resolve old issues.

But not all old issues. My Mom was accepting regarding my sexual preference, as long I didn't tell any of the relatives, her friends or *anyone* that she could possibly have a conversation with in the future, up until the day that she died. She liked Michael but never treated him as a partner of mine, more like a friend.

The Future?

Future plans call for us to gain some equity in our house and then get the hell out of South Florida, a veritable cultural desert. Property values are rising at a ridiculous rate here and our house has already doubled in value in one year. I would like to have a sizable down payment for a small bungalow on the Panhandle or the Jacksonville area. They get three seasons plus a taste of winter there, minus any snow. It's weird, but I long to be cold around December and January.

I've been to London twice and it's been in winter both times, and I usually make at least one trip to NY for Christmas just to get in some Rockefeller Center holiday spirit. I am expecting my first grandchild in July—my foster daughter, Angela and her husband, also a Mike, live in Brooklyn and have been happily married since August, 2002.

I foresee many more trips to NYC in the future. Angela and Mike both love my Michael and include him in everything—including the two of us dancing at their wedding, which was an eye-opener for many of the distant relatives you only see at weddings and funerals.

I've thought for many hours of what I was going to be called by my future grandson/daughter and have decided on Da (Irish) and Michael is going to be La Ti Da, something he hated at first but is definitely getting used to. To my dismay I was misinformed and told that Da referred to Dad. Not being the one who would force my grandchild into an early course of therapy I have decided to be Jagi (Polish) which is what I called my paternal grandfather and what Angela called my dad. Continuity is good in many ways.

No Baggage Allowed

My advice for others in this situation? Leave the baggage at the door, even though that's easier said than done. After my relationship with Tim, it took me a long time to give my trust (thankfully not with Michael). Forget comparisons and don't focus on the crap even though you want to.

Michael

We all have had past relationships, some good, other not. But the night I met Frank, although I was dating someone else at the time, when Frank looked at me and smiled, my world just lit up.

My relationship with Frank has been supportive and loving from the beginning. We have the same likes and dislikes, the same life goals. We've been together for four years, are committed and will be together forever, I absolutely would never let him go.

Frank has such a generous heart. For example, although definitely not a dog lover, when it comes to Ashley, my dog, he has gone out of his way to be kind and loving, he even takes her for her walk first thing every morning. He also never leaves the house in the morning to go to work without a big hug and kiss ... for me! That's the kind of wonderful, thoughtful guy that he is.

Reflections

Often, when someone dies in a tragic way, the grieving may be more complicated. The person may feel unfinished with what he wants to say, since he never had a chance to say goodbye. In this case, the relationship had ended, but that doesn't mean there wasn't a need to grieve. Sometimes there is a delayed grief response. Even troubled relationships have to be mourned and worked through.

Sometimes someone passes away a few years after the relationship has ended and we might even have moved on to a new one, as in the case of Frank and Michael. But, when the old partner passed away, it did bring up a lot of unfinished business that Frank thought he had processed because his relationship with Tim had not been a healthy one. So, upon his passing, Frank revisited this old relationship without all the anger he had felt about Tim when they were together and first broke up. He was able to better appreciate his relationship with his new partner, Michael, and finally heal old feelings about himself and Tim.

Smile at each other, smile at your wife,
smile at your husband, smile at your children,
smile at each other--it doesn't matter who it is—
and that will help you to grow up in greater love
for each other.

Mother Teresa

9.

Marji and Richard

MARJI AND RICHARD seem not only well-suited to each other, but very appreciative that they have found each other. They knew each other over the years because Marji had been a friend to Richard's late wife, Eileen. There is a "special-ness" between them that is evident, they glow in each other's company. They feel lucky and excited that they have "found" each other. They listen well to each other and show a lot of sensitivity toward issues involving extended family. It feels good to be in their presence, there is a good give and take. There is a gentleness that seems evident and under that, a lot of strength. What a pleasure to be in the presence of two happy people who are able to acknowledge their individual worth.

Marji has a bachelor's degree from UCLA in political science and a master's in mythology and depth psychology from Pacifica Graduate Institute in Santa Barbara. She is currently writing her dissertation on the subject of violence and war for her Ph.D. Marji is a journalist, writer and editor, who for many years worked at the *Los Angeles Times* as well as other publications.

Richard is a pharmacist, and owns his own pharmacy. He has been in practice for 40 years, and in the last three years has been semi-retired, working only two days a week. He has two adult children, a daughter who is a year away from being ordained as a Conservative rabbi, and a married son who received his MBA in business administration. He has one 2-year-old grandson.

Marji was divorced for the second time 15 years ago. Her first marriage was for 10 years, the second for 11. She has two grown sons, ages 28 and 34. She and Richard are the same age, or, as Richard jokes, "Marji is older than me by 58 days!"

Richard was married for almost 40 years; a widower for 18 months.

Marji

For a time, Richard and I had been neighbors, living just five houses apart. Richard and Eileen moved into the neighborhood when I was 34 and my eldest son was 3 years old. I was so thrilled to have a playmate for my son. The first thing I could think of was to welcome them with a batch of freshly baked cookies. On meeting Eileen, our connection was instant and close. When we moved away a year or so later, Eileen and I kept in touch. Some years we communicated more often than in others, but we were close friends regardless of distance or time.

We were in the habit of getting together for dinner every three or four weeks; I was working so much until two years ago that it was hard, but we would try for once a month. But I really didn't know Richard very well. Over the years I saw him, of course, at their house and at their New Year's Eve parties and we would chat briefly. I was single by that time.

Ultimately I was with Eileen a lot when she became sick, but when she died I had been away at a conference. I knew she had cancer but didn't have any idea that she would die as soon as she did. When I got back in town, it was a Saturday and I wanted to call her but I would never call a married girlfriend on a Saturday evening and decided to wait until the next day, Sunday. Yet, Saturday night, I just had this compulsion to call. I remember looking at the clock. It was 8:28 p.m. Her sister's boyfriend answered the phone and handed it to Roberta, Eileen's sister.

Roberta said, "Eileen just passed." I couldn't believe it! I was so distraught that the next day, when one of my sons came over, he said, "Let's light every candle in the place. For Eileen." That's how close I was to Eileen. I attended her funeral and called a time or two over the next month. I talked to Deborah, her daughter, and said, "I'm thinking about all of you. Please let your dad know that I called." And I called one other time, just a bereavement call to let them know I was thinking of them.

When Eileen died, in early December, Richard and I had no relationship really, other than through Eileen and that in a tangential way. At the end of April, Richard called to let me know he had found some papers I had written while attending Pacifica College. Eileen was always interested in the papers I wrote during my coursework. Richard said, "I don't know if you want them back, but I didn't want to just get rid of them." I said I would like them back, so he asked if I wanted him to mail them. I said, "No, don't mail them," because the mailman was always putting things in the wrong mailbox at our condo and some of the papers were personal work on *myths of the self*. I certainly didn't want my neighbors getting hold of those.

Richard said, "Why don't we meet for coffee?" And then he added, "Why don't we meet this afternoon?" I was free, so I said okay. As soon as we saw each other, we just broke down; we spent the whole time crying really.

Along with our mutual love for Eileen, we had a lot of history because of our kids. In fact, his son and my older son had been in soccer games together on the same team in grade school. They attended the same private school and were even in the same play. Richard said he had a video of it that I never knew existed. It was really pleasant having this connection. It felt as though I hadn't totally lost Eileen. Richard and I continued to meet for coffee … I had no idea what I was getting into.

Lean on Me

We had known each other at this point for 31 years. Richard was in a grief support group when we started having coffee. It was seven months after Eileen died that we officially started going together. I think the support group was very helpful for him. On the other hand, there were times when it was a little hard on me, because I wasn't actually in the group.

I was just about always in therapy for my own growth. And certainly that helped. In my own case I think I did my grieving before I left the marriages that I was in. I didn't want to end my marriages as failures. After all my therapy, the second time around, I married the one guy that my therapist said could not be "therapized." He actually said that to me. Yet I believe in therapy. I was going to write a book called *The Girl Who Loved Group Therapy*. I really do believe in the growth process: growth, education and development are so important to me. Therapy did help me to resolve my divorce issues. The reality is that all my money, all my life has gone to therapy and education.

In terms of my own life, I experienced a great deal of shame as a child because of my parents; my father battered my mother, and the neighbors called the police and all that sort of thing. So I had this goal on a subconscious level of having a perfect marriage. When my marriages ended, I felt like a real failure even though my first husband's psychiatrist said to me, 'Why do you stay?' And that was a startling question to me. I don't think that I could have gotten beyond all of the grief and shame and could not have blossomed, as my life has continued to blossom, without therapy. I think counseling is just fundamental to the well-lived life.

The hardest time during my two failed marriages was before I left rather than after. That is when a great deal of my mourning took place, especially in the marriage that produced my two sons. At the time, they were three and nine years old and it was very hard to leave their father. But my husband had a bipolar disorder and wouldn't stick with anything that could help—I really had to leave but the hardest part was breaking up the family, and being very frightened financially. I felt like I might never be attractive to men again; and that was my feeling at the end of both marriages. Because each of my marriages lasted for about a decade, Richard has pointed out that I am on the "10-year-plan."

Divorce is Loss Too

In leaving my children's father, I was around 40 and played into that societal conditioning that I was *so* old. I didn't date for a long time, but I got the family involved in the Unitarian Church and that was really healing to me. I had a few brief relationships but I was very interested in not breaking anyone in with my children at that point.

After the last marriage, to my children's stepfather, I went on a sabbatical from men. And I've pretty much been on that sabbatical for a long time. This hiatus was really quite important and wonderful for me, and lasted for about another 12 years. I'd had a few dates here and there, but I really didn't have sexual relationships. I didn't want to have a serious relationship until I got my 14-year-old son raised and launched.

Starting Over

I didn't start dating Richard because I was desperately lonely. Oh no! When I started this relationship with Richard I was so happy with my life. It was so full. I'd finally worked through all that stuff about feeling like I only had a half-life when I wasn't with a guy. Although I do feel that we're made to be in a partnership if possible, by this time I knew it would have to be pretty high-toned and positive. So maybe I learned some lessons. Actually, a few years before Richard and I got together, I began to get my head straight, feeling positive about men in general where before, I had been rather negative about men.

When I was attending Pacifica College, aside from the academic, in my own work on personal myths, I discovered that I was living in the wrong myth. The old myth worked well for me as a child – perhaps the myth of Athena, the warrior, always brave and helpful to the hero, but living through the man. As a child, I became sort of the mediator in the family. I was the youngest and the only one that wasn't beaten. So I was the one who intervened with my father, saying 'Don't hurt Mama tonight; and be nice to Brucie tonight,' my older brother.

So with the work I'd done at Pacifica College, I realized that part of me didn't want to have a relationship again. That was always way back in my mind. While it would have been great to have a wonderful relationship, I had sort of written it off, at least for the near future, because I had other things I wanted to accomplish that were important to me. And I was proud that I did that. And then I realized, there are some amazing, wonderful men teaching at Pacifica. Of course, not available, but it gave me the idea that there are some great guys out there. And I realized just how really biased I was. I realized that if I ever wanted to attract a wonderful man, I had to change *my* attitude.

Not one to go out searching for men, on the Internet or otherwise, I sent up a little prayer. And I said, "You know, God, I'd sure like somebody great. I know I'm doing my dissertation all the time. But, you know what? If you want me to have somebody, send him in. But I'm not going out looking."

Richard and I feel that we were meant to be. Initially going to coffee we were just friends and both grieving for Eileen. I certainly wasn't grieving to the degree that Richard was but we really commiserated. Richard cried, and we would sit at the Coffee Bean. I remember saying to my 89 year old mother, "You know, Richard and I have been having coffee and it's kind of weird. We're kind of friends, but we're now also having lunch here and there. We have a lot in common and enjoy each other." My mother answered, "No, it's not weird at all! That's how you meet people."

Friends First

We were definitely friends first. My mother suggested that I bring Richard a casserole because that's what people in her age group do for widowers. I said, "That is so tacky. I would never take him a casserole." Finally I said to my mother, "Well, you know, I guess we're just going to have coffee for a long time together. It doesn't seem to be stepping up or whatever."

All of a sudden, she said, "You know, some little blonde's going to grab him." And I said, "Well, mom, you know, I guess if he wants a little blonde, he'll just go there, you know." I was really terribly annoyed by that comment. And it kept bothering me for several days. And then I thought, well, this is supposed to be the age of equality. I *can* invite him to dinner.

A week later I invited him to come to dinner at my house. Just kind of casual, you know. And I said to him, "Isn't that what you're supposed to do with widowers, invite them?" And he was somewhat offended by that. But I was trying to make a little disclaimer: Don't get me wrong, I'm not trying to be too aggressive here. Who the hell knows what to do at this point in your life? I mean, he hasn't dated. Well, Thursday or Friday before our Sunday dinner, I was talking with a friend and said, "You know, I think I'm going to seduce the hell out of him." So anyway, I just kind of got with the program then.

I started figuring out a great little upscale dinner. I wore my lavender satin top that showed a little cleavage and my black velvet pants. I called Richard to see what kind of wine he would like, and maybe that gave him a little clue. I don't know. But anyway, I had this wonderful dinner planned. I went to the Farmer's Market that morning to get fresh scallions for the orange roughy I'd planned to cook.

As it turned out I was running late when he got there and I couldn't find the scallions, and I was in a panic thinking: *What am I going to do?* So I decided to use garlic and he decided to help me with the garlic. He worked while sitting in my kitchen on the stool, and I was so self-conscious because he was watching me. I was really quite nervous at this point, much to my surprise. I've been cooking for years and years.

It was a nice dinner. The final touch was chocolate dipped strawberries. Later Richard told me that dessert (plus the candles and Simon & Garfunkel music) were the clues that tipped him off.

That was seven months ago to the day. In some ways, it's an odd feeling, having known Eileen, but on the other hand, we have a lot in common. My mother keeps reminding me that it's okay to have a relationship with somebody whose wife you knew and who has passed away. In my whole life I haven't really listened to my mother – until now.

On With the New

In every, wonderful way, Richard is different from my past husband. First of all, Richard has been in therapy for a decade or two. Plus he went through grief counseling, which was really a great thing. Thankfully his background enabled him to go into his feelings to experience the grief and to have the strength to take off from work and to just be with himself, to live with his feelings. He really loved Eileen and they had a great marriage, even though I know they had ups and downs and major issues from time to time. Because we'd been girlfriends I knew some of those things.

We both came to this relationship with a lot of background and ability to work things through, talk things through, put things on the table, to accept things about each other's realities and backgrounds and children. I think that Richard is just a wonderful, wonderful man, and I feel really blessed to have him in my life. Because of our past experiences, I think we're able to be at a much deeper level. It's really genuine. I've wanted that my whole life, and who knew. It's like magic.

A Fear of Flying

Being emotionally vulnerable again was very scary, even though it felt very natural. At first my attitude was: It feels good now, but what if it doesn't last? Trying to protect myself, I remember telling my friends that it's a great summer romance because it started in July. Now it's Richard who reminds me when issues come up, "Don't pull away from me; stay with it, work on it." He's the most consciously aware guy I've been with. It's really wonderful. Plus he has a great sense of humor. Preparing to be sexual again was also a hurdle to overcome.

I've never been an overweight person really, but my weight was up at that time. I hadn't been doing any exercise because of work demands and so I started going to the gym, went on the South Beach Diet, and lost 27 pounds. I was really into looking good and feeling good, even buying new clothes after not shopping for a decade. I started wearing colorful things and jewelry I hadn't worn for a long time. I got into my aphrodisiac self. I was feeling pretty good about myself, about my body, and that was a good thing because I don't know if I would have encouraged this relationship otherwise. I was back to being myself, the way I had always been when I was younger. And so it was just a really amazing and beautiful moment.

The idea of intimacy came naturally, but the fact of it was new. I love intimacy. But I had been away from it for a long time, and I didn't want to get hooked. I wanted to become intimate, and yet, it's impossible to be intimate without becoming vulnerable. So I was going to take it slowly, I thought. Ha! Within a week of our becoming intimate we were living together. And it's been really beautiful. It's been great. But not without initial apprehension.

I was worried about vaginal dryness and all the other menopause symptoms, but finally, not many months before Richard and I got together, I had gotten my hormones balanced with something that really worked. I had tried all the post-menopausal creams and all that kind of stuff which, for me, did not work. Finally I tried a progesterone and estradiol cream compounded just for me and it worked. So physically, intimacy wasn't a problem. It was beautiful. I'm shy, but we were able to talk about our expectations.

The reality is that it was like going back to feeling like an adolescent again; the whole romantic thing. Richard was very, very attractive to me. I think there was a lot of chemistry by that point. It wasn't just somebody I was going to go to bed with for the hell of it.

Enter, the Family

Our few problems had to do with his children, mostly. And even that wasn't so much directed at me personally. They liked me. They'd known me somewhat from the past. Unlike my own children though, they just weren't used to a broken family. They adored their parents; they had a beautiful family. They were just in shock and quite vocal. They're very strong-willed children who had a lot of power in the family; the power dynamics of the family without Eileen changed radically.

His kids are still having trouble with Richard and I being together. They were not nice to Richard. Their comments were really harsh and angry. And I felt bad for him and I was afraid they were going to influence him to not have a relationship with me. When I think back to that time, I have to admit that it was really hard sometimes.

I'm not even sure that our timing had anything to do with it. I have a feeling that if it had been a year and a half, they would still have had the same issues. They see me in this house, and that is hard for them. However, I think they have had too much power in determining their father's life and their parents' lives.

For a long time, with me it was, "I've just got to go home. I've got to be at my place with my stuff." Richard's house felt like a shrine to their marriage and the kids would notice if some things had been moved. But Richard has been wonderful. That's what has made it work; he knows enough to make our relationship primary. And he is so caring of his kids. But if he had capitulated to their wishes in this way or that, I don't know if I could have handled it. Lately there's a shift and things have moved somewhat in the right direction, but there are angry periods too. Richard's son and daughter-in-law are still angry, but his daughter and I have started a nice relationship. We can talk; she's had a lot of therapy herself. She's a very feminist kind of gal, she's articulate. She's also well educated, reads a lot. In fact she's made comments to Richard on my behalf that are very positive, about things that we have in common.

I think it's very tricky when you come into someone's life when they are still grieving. And the children are still grieving and I don't know when that stops. But I do think I handled it the best I could. I don't know what else I could have done.

I had my feelings, but I didn't act out or vocalize them to the kids or take pot shots because of some of the remarks I was hearing. I always tried to come at things from their point of view.

Support for Whom?

I have some feelings about the grief support group Richard attended. When there was some kind of get-together socially, for example Labor Day, even though we were well into the relationship, only Richard would be invited. The rule as I heard it was that outsiders don't get to go and I was really angry about it. I felt that no one was caring about me. After so many months, I began feeling like, *Where am I in all this?* That's the hard part.

And sometimes, Richard would start crying about Eileen. And I loved Eileen, but it was like: What does that mean? And I would have to just go home. One night we went to the theatre. The play, *Carolyn or Change*, oddly enough was about a widower who got together with his wife's friend, a surprise to both of us. Well, by the time the play was over and we were driving home, Richard is crying and really missing Eileen and this was supposed to have been a special evening for us.

This was the first time I let myself just express what I felt, which was "pissed off." And I said, "You know what, you need to go home and be in that house with Eileen and just leave me off;" and that's what he did. And I was mad. Well, we were on the phone twenty minutes later, talking and I ended up back at his house where we had always been together. But, it was good for me to really express how angry that made me. Even though I felt at the same time, poor guy he's grieving. So we can have those kinds of moments here and there.

Monday Morning Quarterback

I don't know what I would have done differently, but I have thought about that a lot. I think the fact that I am this age, that I am well-seasoned in life, that I've had a lot of therapy, that I love kids, has helped. Our kids are of the same age range and I care about his kids and I loved Eileen, I still loved Eileen. It's been confusing in that way. I don't think I could have handled this at a younger age. One important ingredient is that Richard has been so *there* in our relationship, and so respectful of us and me, at the same time. I think he's the one who has probably had the hardest time, being caught in the middle. As far as his kids, they were sometimes disrespectful of him before Eileen died, but she was there to mediate.

I'm kind of proud that I have had enough therapy that I can step back and not get vocal. I let the kids be what they have to be, sometimes angry and pissed off. Of course they miss their mother and of course it's hard that I'm here in this role, although I'm not trying to replace their mother. We were careful about that. Also, Richard has been open about our relationship. I feel if he had been sneaky about it, it would have fed the problem.

Only in the last few weeks, Richard has said, "Why don't you make one of the rooms your office?" because I'm having a hard time with all my books and finding a place where I can study. The worst thing for me is the disorientation. Where am I supposed to live? On weekends, we go out to the beach, where Richard keeps an apartment, and then I'm the all-time shlepper. Yet how can I complain when I have this richness, even though it's a little disorienting some times?

The Engines That Could

I want to keep this going. I want to spend my life with him in whatever way that is going to be. We don't know. It's rather new. At a year and a month it feels very good.

Richard

I was surrounded by helpful friends and family when Eileen died. My brother, he was amazing, as far as being there for me. We'd go out, we'd talk. He'd be with me. I have a place at the beach. He'd come down for the weekend and stay with me. My nephew was there for me. My workout partner was there. My kids were also very available. I had support from one of my technicians at work. And later, I attended a bereavement support group for about eight months.

I Hear You

The group was another avenue of expression for my feelings, and also a way to connect to, and be supported by, other people going through the same process—hearing them helped to clarify my process. For the most part it was a very positive experience. In the end, I felt that a lot of people were stuck in the same place and that I had grown beyond them and didn't feel the need to stay in the group any longer.

In the beginning, shortly after Eileen's death, my life was totally upside down. I didn't know which end was up. That was for the first couple of months especially. I did have the wisdom *not* to go back to work for a month. And I decided – and I said to myself, "I want to feel everything. I'm not going to block anything. I want everything to come in and everything to go out. And I'm just going to get through this process in time." And I just knew I would. I just didn't know who I was anymore. I knew everything in my life had been going well, pretty much. And now, I just didn't know shit.

It was so confusing in the beginning, because I didn't know who I was or what I was; a lot of my life was who I was in relationship to my spouse. And all of a sudden, I didn't have a spouse. I had my kids. But they weren't around that much really. My daughter stayed with me. She'd been in Israel in August, before Eileen died. I called her in September to let her know that Eileen had taken a turn for the worse and it was serious. She came home and she stayed with us until Eileen died in December. She stayed with me for another three weeks after Eileen died and then left.

Some Things Don't Pay

I *never* felt as if I dated. I did see someone one time, after Eileen's death. Someone who I just felt I could have a sexual relationship with who I met when I went away for a weekend at Esalen Institute. So I told my daughter, and I told my nephew, and I told my brother. I told them that

I'd "met this lady. I know it's a transitional relationship. She lives in another city. Maybe I'll see her once in a while." This was in February or March, something like that.

Well, that was like a major disaster. Oh God! Sometimes it just doesn't pay to get laid at all. That's the bottom-line. This woman fell out of my bed at four in the morning and broke two ribs that later punctured her lung. She damn near died. She was in the hospital for 16 days. She had blood clots on her lung. And I went into a two-week depression and turmoil that was just a god-awful time. But I stayed with her in terms of giving her support through the whole thing. It was just a horrendous experience.

People wanted to fix me up, and I just wasn't interested. I had a lot of people who'd say, "I've got just a great woman for you." But I knew that I would find someone when I was ready. I just knew it. Eileen had told me, "You're not the kind of man that can live alone. You need to be with a woman." And I just knew that I wouldn't have any trouble finding a woman. And as it turns out, I didn't, as luck would have it.

Dating? What's That?

The interesting thing is that I wasn't looking for anything. I never did date. Or I never considered myself as having dated. I remember the only time that I felt lonely after Eileen's death was on Mother's Day. We had a brunch over at the house and then everybody left. And I just didn't know what to do with myself. I ended up going to the cemetery.

But I didn't start seeing Marji out of loneliness. I wasn't looking for anything. I just remembered that Marji was a great person. I always loved her as a person and thought that she was really special. I just wanted to return the papers she'd lent Eileen to read. I didn't feel comfortable reading them because I knew they were personal and we didn't have a relationship then.

At about that time, I felt I was coming out of this dark cloud I'd been under for the last couple years. I was working things out at this point and coming out of this gloom that began well before Eileen died. It was right around that time that I discovered these papers and I called Marji, and we went out for coffee. It had been about five months since Eileen died.

Just a Perfect Blend-ship

Friendship was there from the start. Let's put it this way. We went out that first time for coffee. An hour later I said, "You know, Marji, I think we could be friends. Actually, Marji, we are friends." What I meant was that we could talk very easily. And Marji's a great listener. She can really be there.

At the same time, this friendship didn't change the way I felt about Eileen. I don't think it's impacted it in any way whatsoever. I still love Eileen and remember things about her. But maybe I could have handled things differently with my children. Actually, I told my kids,

"You know, Marji's a lot easier to get along with than Mom," and they did not like it. Not too tactful! I blew it a few times along the way! Actually, Eileen was a more effusive kind of person. I mean she was more volatile than Marji, but she was a great partner too. I've been really blessed to have two great partners.

Not Peas in a Pod

Eileen and Marji are different not just in personality, but in appearance. They are different body types, I guess. Eileen was shorter. Marji has better legs. Different color hair. These differences haven't impacted our relationship. I appreciate both women for the way they are.

Becoming emotionally vulnerable again was not at all scary. I was just thinking of Marji's invitation for dinner. I'm coming into Marji's place for the first time, and I had never been to her place. I was very calm and relaxed. I'm sitting there in her kitchen, and she's like all nervous and everything. And I'm just looking at her. And she's talking about Eros, you know, and the wine's there, and the music, and the candles. But it's like *she's* slipping and sliding away. So I thought, *there is something going on here.* At that point we were just friends, I hadn't considered anything else. In fact, when I was at Esalen, I even told my instructor's wife about Marji, saying, "You know, I just have no idea about what's going to happen with Marji because we're friends." And she cautioned, "Well, just take it very slowly" because she and her husband had dated for years before getting married. They were younger then, and I guess they had kids that they were each raising. Well, our kids were grown. So I took it slowly until that night, and then we picked up the pace. Becoming physically intimate was very comfortable. I can say this: I think we have amazing sex. I have never been with anyone where, two-thirds of the time we have orgasms together. It's amazing. The reality is that I'm pretty secure in myself and my sexuality. And Marji is too.

This part of the relationship developed easily, without any expectations on my part. I didn't even realize I was being seduced until I finally kind of figured it out. Marji brushed against my foot before dinner. Afterward she said, "Oh, I'm sorry, it was an accident." I replied, "There are no accidents in the universe, Marji." And then I kicked my shoe off and started playing footsie with her during dinner.

Double Trouble

I think the only argument that we've ever really had – well, maybe there were two, were about silly things; about tooth brushing and a towel, and the other was about Marji being on time. That was our biggest argument. But outside of that, I think the major thing was the kids impinging on us somewhat. And Marji needed a lot of reassurance from me that she was primary, although I told her right from the get-go that, "Nobody's going to get in the way of our relationship." Even though things didn't always go smoothly, it was fine. It just developed.

My kids, unfortunately, felt differently. My kids were furious with me for being with another person. And it was expressed *overtly*. There was a lot of hostility shot in my direction; especially from my daughter in the beginning.

I remember sitting with Marji and my daughter in my kitchen, talking about my giving Marji a pair of Eileen's earrings. And Marji wanted to clarify that with Deborah who said, "I know that this is my problem, the negative way I feel about your wearing my mother's jewelry, because at the same time, I really like you, Marji." And then, months later, Marji and I were together with my daughter at her place and she told us about a dream in which Eileen had come to her, telling her all about the things that she missed about being with me. But she also added, "Now, its Marji's turn." And that marked a big turning point for the three of us.

And Later?

I have a very good life with this lady, Marji. I had felt for a long time that I had had no joy in my life. Marji has really brought me joy. She's a real blessing to me and I'm grateful for what we have. My recommendation to others is this: Just be open to feel your feelings, work through them and sort them out. And know that it's going to take time and for some people, it takes longer than others. Be open to anything coming your way.

Marji can be open and forthright and expressive in her feelings towards Richard and his family. She has shown tremendous sensitivity for understanding their issues, including the difficulties in dating a widowed man whose children were not ready to have that happen. Grown children grieve on their own timetable and it is clearly different than their parent. They are usually resentful of dating that starts too soon (in their eyes). They want their parent to be happy, but they also are activated emotionally when they are reminded that they've lost their mother or father. As Marji said, "I think it's very tricky when you come into someone's life when they are still grieving."

Fortunately, there was a lot of discussion, a lot of attempts to understand other people's feelings and to work with that. Thankfully both Richard and Marji have each had a lot of counseling in their backgrounds and are truly evolved people who are caring about each other and their families.

They want to work out the family problems while also maintaining something special between them. They both honored Eileen's presence and influence, and at the same time, they are trying to develop a life for themselves. It took hard work, understanding, patience and sensitivity. They are both well educated in their respective fields, both employ a great sense of humor and tremendous willingness to have happiness, to not give up, and to work things out. It is delightful to be in their presence. They not only show high regard for each other but offer a lot of gentleness and rapport, while underneath, there is the strength to make this successful.

Love is sometimes denied, sometimes lost,
sometimes unrecognized, but in the end,
always found with no regrets, forever valued
and kept treasured.

Author Unknown

10.

Elaine & Hy

HY IS OUTGOING and personable, gracious and charming. His late wife was a homemaker, while Elaine was manager of a Bank Savings and Loan for 13 years before becoming a homemaker. Elaine and Hy have been married for eight months. They are obviously very happy, glad that they have found one another. They share a love of staying fit, Hy with his running and Elaine with her walking. Both look younger than their chronological age of 74. And they seem genuinely happy. Hy likes that Elaine is fit, that she caters to his needs, and makes him feel important.

In Hy's words, Elaine is "beautiful, caring, loving, and extremely considerate of my feelings. She knows when I'm hurting. She is wonderful with my sons, daughters-in-law and grandchildren. Although I was married for 45 years, the reality is that I share more of my feelings with Elaine than I did with my late wife. Toward the end of her life, I became more impatient with her, not as loving as I was at one time. I was tired of being a caregiver. I wondered, 'Is this the way it will be for the rest of my life?' and became a little selfish."

In return, Elaine says, "Hy is a very caring, communicative, and a sentimental person. He's very easy to live with, has an even keel, and doesn't fly off the handle. Doesn't get upset. We communicate a lot; the relationship is very easy."

Elaine was married for 48 years; her husband passed away a little over five years ago. Hy had been married for 45 years; his wife passed away five and a half years ago.

Elaine

In some ways, I feel that my friends let me down after my husband died. Most of my friends were not as wonderful as I had hoped, although there were a few couples that stuck with me and saw to it I wasn't alone during the bad times. With my other friends, I was extremely disappointed. They just kind of forgot that I was alive until I was part of a couple again. It was very sad.

My family, including my sister-in-law and brothers-in-law, on my husband's side were, and continue to be, wonderful. We are still very close and they saw to it that I had something to do on Sunday's and other difficult days.

About two months after my late husband, Norm's, death, I began attending a grief support group at the urging of two friends who had lost spouses. They insisted I go for at least three meetings and after taking me the first time, I went by myself. It was pretty hard but it also helped me so much. At that time I was not in good shape emotionally.

Just sitting in the support group and listening to other people with the same problems, the same experiences that I had, was comforting. Slowly I began to talk to the people in my group, making dear and lasting friendships. Because they understood what I was going through, I was able to talk freely. It helped a lot because I didn't need to hold my pain inside, which is not a good thing. The group experience made me more aware.

Doing Hard Time

My two daughters live out of town. Initially they stayed with me, but when they left, I was alone in my condo. My late husband's clothes were gone because, when the girls were there, they felt they should take care of getting rid of them with me and I agreed. That was painful, and then being alone added to my pain.

I'd had a husband who did everything; he was just very able and willing to do all kinds of things. I didn't even know how to pump gas, until the very end when he was sick, because that's what he did. There were so many 'firsts' after his passing. For example, I drove by myself to visit a friend about an hour or so out of town. It took four different freeways to get there. Because of all the interchanges between freeways, I allowed about two hours to get there. It was very difficult, but I did it. Another example was taking my car in for service. I am ashamed to admit that I didn't even know how to put air in my tires.

One of the saddest things for me, it sounds funny now when I think about it, was that every time I saw an RV on the street, I would get hysterical. My husband and I had so many good years traveling in one, just the two of us. Now, of course, I see an RV and I think that was my other life and this is my new life and I'm fine.

Social Needs

It took a while to begin dating again. At first I certainly wasn't ready at all. It was about eight months, maybe even a year, before I started going out at all. It was hard. I hadn't made small talk in a long time and even the thought of having to do that was scary.

I began to date because I like the company of a male and I needed somebody just to talk to, or go out to dinner with, or go out with to a play or museum, or whatever. It had nothing to do with intimacy at that time.

I met Hy in our grief support group. We talked, but that was about it. Hy began dating another woman, and I went on my way, meeting some wonderful people, women and men who became dear friends. About four and a half years later, I heard from a mutual friend that Hy was single again. By then I was also no longer seeing the man that I had been dating. Our mutual friend suggested that I meet him and Hy at 5:30 one morning before their twice-weekly walk.

I went to the park at 5:30 but I couldn't find them because it was still dark outside, so I went home. The next time we spoke, I asked where exactly they met. The next time, I found them, but immediately tripped and fell on the sidewalk. It was not pretty. Anyway, the next time we met during their morning walk, we made a date and that was it. Hy asked me to go to dinner that Sunday night, we went to see a show in Beverly Hills and we have been together ever since. Our relationship progressed quickly. We knew we had much in common, yet were no longer kids, so we didn't want to waste a lot of time.

Him and Him

This new relationship has nothing to do with my feelings for my late spouse. My late spouse was then and my feelings for him haven't changed. My feelings for Hy are just different. This is our second chance at happiness and our life is a different life.

Although my late husband was handy around the house, as well as Hy, being able to fix anything, socially and recreationally into sports, they are a little different. It doesn't matter what Hy and I are doing; we just like to be together. Hy is an easy person.

My deceased husband was a golfer who used to play football for Michigan. He went to every sports thing in the world and I learned to play golf because of him. We played a lot of golf all over the country and it was wonderful. We made many good friends that way, friends that I still see. I gave the game up two years ago; it had nothing to do with Hy, I just got tired of it. Norm had also been very into charity work, running golf tournaments and served as president of various associations while I was the treasurer.

Into the Void

I was apprehensive about becoming emotionally vulnerable again, but scared would be too strong a word. I'd already had one relationship that lasted a year before Hy and I got together, so although becoming physically intimate with Hy was something I thought about, it wasn't scary. In my previous relationship, I had known this man for forty years; I had been best friends with his wife. *That* was scary *because* we knew each other so well. Society's expectations regarding sex have nothing to do with me. Absolutely, nothing. And they didn't affect anything. My outlook was this: Whatever happened, happened. I didn't expect anything special, anything different. Hy and I didn't talk about our expectations, nor had I discussed sexuality with my first husband.

Any Problems?

We've had no problems; we've been very lucky. I only wish we'd met a few years earlier. Other than that, so far it's wonderful.

My entire family has been outstanding; no problems at all. We are very, very lucky. I'm hoping for many happy and healthy years; I hope we continue on for at least 20 years. When we were younger, my late husband and I had some money problems, as did most young couples ... I was the "hamburger queen." Hy and I don't have to deal with that now.

My advice to others is just to hang in there and accept that you'll never forget your late spouse but that you have to get on with your life and that it will be 'just different'. Accept that while you had a wonderful life before, once it's gone; don't hole yourself up in a room with a sheet over your head. You have life ahead of you and you should enjoy it, as best you can.

Hy

After my wife died, my friends were fairly considerate, but my family was much more supportive because they were also grieving. Friends were supportive just at the beginning, for maybe a couple of months after the loss of my spouse. I found it so much more helpful to attend a bereavement support group. To paraphrase friends, their comments of "I know how you feel," and "Time is going to heal," didn't help because they really didn't know how I felt. The bereavement group members knew how I felt because they were going through the same feelings as I. I found that very supportive and looked forward to our Thursday night meetings, which I attended for 9 months. I left because I started dating a woman from the group. We enjoyed being together and I felt guilty going back to the group after they knew that we were seeing each other; I didn't want them to see me being as happy as I was while the other members were still hurting.

The most important factor in helping my grief was realizing that other people were in the same position that I was. I remember Elaine when she attended, her pain and sadness. Yet, I also remember her going alone that first time to visit some friends out of town and how supportive the group was.

I remember the first time I decided to go to Cambria, California, by myself, a place that had been one of my late wife's and my favorite vacation spots. I went by myself on a weekend. When I got back, the group wanted to know how I did and how I survived it; they were so supportive. It was absolutely wonderful.

Oh, Those First Months

Those first few months alone, adapting to being alone, were very hard. I was a caregiver for many years, willingly. It was hard sleeping alone at night, tossing in bed alone ... not being able to go out to a restaurant and ask for a table for one. I couldn't go to a restaurant that had tablecloths; I could go to a deli or a coffee shop. Rose and I went to so many restaurants; and I couldn't go back to those alone. I found that very difficult.

In the beginning, I found it very difficult sleeping at night. I found it very difficult cleaning the house and giving away the clothes, even with the help of my children. It was an awful time.

Transitions

I guess I was more fortunate than most people, because about four months into my grieving, I met a woman in the bereavement support group that I asked out to dinner. She lived in the neighborhood and we started dating. It made life easier, more pleasant ... that we were able to go out to restaurants or a show and so on, all this while trying to keep our relationship secret. In fact, one of our first dates was for a musical on Sunset Boulevard in Hollywood and, just my luck, we ran into the director of our bereavement support group at the theater.

I think I needed intimacy. Because of my late wife's illness, for a long time we had no real intimacy. I needed someone to share feelings with, I needed someone to talk to ... I just didn't think it would happen that quickly. Although when Rose knew that she was dying, she encouraged me to see a therapist and not to wait. In fact, Rose had been seeing a therapist right before she passed away and the therapist called me after she died and said, "I need to talk to you."

I told the therapist that I didn't want to talk to her. I said, "I'm OK." She came to my house anyway and she said, "I need to tell you something. When Rose was dying, she wanted me to tell you how much she loved you and how wonderful the marriage was. But she also wanted me to tell you that it is okay to date, and not to wait." The therapist asked if I had any feelings about that. Oh God, I could cry now, just remembering our conversation. I told her that, yes, I knew Rose's wishes, but to hear someone else tell me that, it gave me permission. Rose's feelings were not a surprise to me because I would have said the same thing to her. I would have wanted her to be happy, just as she wanted the same thing for me.

Then, Elaine

I met Elaine through our bereavement support group, although when we first met I was seeing someone else and after awhile, she was seeing someone else. Although we were friendly with each other and enjoyed talking, that was it. We had a good feeling for each other but went our different ways. Unfortunately, it took four and a half years for us to get together, that's how life is.

Other than our meeting at our bereavement support group and then going our separate ways, we were not really friends. We later met again through a mutual friend who knew that she had ended her relationship and that I had ended mine. He encouraged her to come out to meet us. However, even if he hadn't called to invite her to join our early morning walk, I was ready to call her. I did think of her over the years and found her to be very attractive. I knew that she had had a long term marriage, as I had had, and there was something about her that attracted me.

My feelings for my late spouse haven't changed. Elaine and I have the kind of marriage where we talk about our spouses freely; there will be a song on the radio, a place that we go to and Elaine will say, "Norman and I used to go there," or I will say, "Rose and I used to go there." Something will happen, we sometimes well up with tears of some reminder, but I think we have such a strong loving relationship that it's okay to do that. Still, they are two different people.

Elaine is much healthier than Rose was; she likes to have a drink with me, which Rose never did. We like to travel. Elaine is much thinner and healthier than Rose, it's just a different marriage, yet as loving as my first marriage was.

I don't think this marriage has anything to do with my first marriage to Rose; having been married before hasn't made a difference at all. This is a new life, a new beginning. I feel blessed and so lucky that Elaine and I did get together, that we have this opportunity to have this wonderful relationship.

Bed Time Stories

It was very scary to become emotionally vulnerable. Number one, I thought I would never get married again, although right after Rose died, everyone wanted to fix me up with someone. For some reason, they thought, hey, he's a pretty good catch. But, when I met Elaine, I think I knew from the beginning it was going to be a lasting relationship. I didn't know it was going to be marriage until we started dating ... almost every night from our first date on.

Exploring the physical side of it wasn't scary at all. It was different, it was a different person. Rose had been very loving and very passionate, and I found the same thing with Elaine. I found she was very giving, and very loving and passionate. I think because we loved each other, it was not as difficult as I thought it would be.

Because I was in relationship prior to seeing Elaine, it was easier for me to experience sexual intimacy with someone other than my late wife. And I think it was easier for Elaine also because, although we never discussed this, she had been in a prior relationship after her husband died.

Quite frankly, the first relationship after my wife's death was very difficult and scary. Elaine and I never talked about that because it never came up in our relationship. Sexual intimacy was part of our relationship almost from the beginning, in a very loving, caring, giving way. It had been scary during my first relationship because it had been a long time since I had relations with my wife due to her illness. I didn't know what my feelings would be, I didn't know whether I could perform the way I wanted to, or whether I could satisfy someone.

I don't think there were any unrealistic expectations. I just wanted to have pleasure, try to, perhaps, recapture some of my youth. I found that my partner was very giving and loving and made it very easy for me to have a relationship.

Sex is Easy. Talk is Hard

I don't think we talked about sex or our expectations. I think we both knew that we cared for each other. I don't think it could have been a relationship without our loving each other. I didn't want just a sexual relationship. I think that could have been very easy to do with just anyone, and that's not what I wanted. I wanted a lasting, committed relationship. The sexuality was just a natural evolution.

We were fortunate in having no real problems to overcome. There were absolutely no bumps at all. It has been loving from then until now. We had no problems whatsoever.

My only wish is that Elaine and I had gotten together initially and not wasted those five years without each other. Although, maybe it wouldn't have worked then. Maybe we wouldn't have been ready at that time. But, I feel now that five years was a long time and that we could have had that much more happiness.

Family Blessing

We're both lucky that our families were and are very, very happy for both of us. Now, my vision is to take care of Elaine, to love her and have a wonderful, wonderful life.

I don't know if I'm in a position to offer advice to others, but I think you have to have an open and honest relationship with your new partner, to not hold back, as when you were young. I think you have to not have any secrets, just love each other and never go to bed mad; to kiss goodbye every morning and kiss goodnight every night; and, be very considerate of each other.

Elaine is beautiful, she is caring, she is loving. She is extremely considerate of my feelings. She knows when I'm hurting and thinking of Rose and when that comes up, she talks about Rose to me. She is wonderful with my sons, daughters-in-law and grandchildren. I just couldn't ask for anything better.

Reflections

Elaine and Hy seem very well suited to each other. They both look outward at the same things. They share a love of fitness and value of family. They recognize that the early years of establishing a family and making one's way in the world are past them. They appreciate that they can reap the benefits of enjoying financial security, travel and good times. They genuinely care for each other as well as love each other. Hy was married a long time to an ill wife, so he appreciates that Elaine is fit and active and wants it to stay that way. She takes good care of him in many small ways and he shows pleasure in taking care of her.

They both had previous relationships, so it makes their coming together as a couple even sweeter for them. They enjoy life and recognize how fortunate they have been to find mates that complement each other well.

The life and love we create is the life and love we live.
Leo Buscaglia

11.

Tobie & Richard

RICHARD AND TOBIE are interesting as individuals and as a couple. Both have been married twice, and they have five children between them. Tobie has a doctorate in education-learning theory; both are members of the Plato Society and thoroughly enjoy the research and presentation of topics involved; they are highly intellectual and appreciate intellectual stimulation. As a couple, they enjoy reading and research. Tobie has many degrees, and many interests that continue in her retirement. She enjoyed an exciting life of travel with her second husband.

Richard was in the men's retail business. He had always had a girlfriend or dated a lot but never had a relationship that embraced an emotional commitment. Tobie and Richard seem to appreciate each other for where they are now in their lives and the interests that they are able to share. They openly admire one another, adding a spark to each other's life.

Tobie has a master's degree, a doctorate, and a Marriage and Family Counseling license. "I have various licenses and have had various careers," said Tobie," but never a long-term one."

Tobie was married to her second husband for thirty-five years; she has been a widow for two and a half. Richard has been married twice, once for 20 years, the second time for 15; he has been a widower for two.

Tobie

My daughter Teri, who lives locally, has been, for many, many years, the person I'm closest to, along with my sister. Teri was the one who really held everything together and gave me the support system I needed to keep things running smoothly. We spoke twice a day. She works full-time, but she would call me on the way to work and on her way home.

During my grieving, I didn't think it appropriate to feel sorry for myself since my husband was the one who had to die. I cried most when I watched a TV program that we used to watch together ... one that he would have enjoyed. I was never lonely because I allowed myself to do something I had never really done before. I read novels as much as I wanted to, which was a great deal of the time. I often could not do paperwork that I really needed to do because I knew I couldn't concentrate. I went out with friends because I knew it was unhealthy not to do so, but I built a nest out of the comfort of my books.

Now Richard is my best support; he is one of the most very important people in my life.

I tried attending a grief support group, but went only three times. I did not feel that it was a comfortable place for me. I am very, very open, but the facilitator of this particular group was a non-take-charge person; she was unable to direct the group in a positive way. And, since I am also a therapist, though I haven't practiced it much, I found myself rescuing her, and didn't feel that I was getting enough out of it. Before my husband died, I had started seeing a therapist because I knew that I probably should be seeing someone I could be talking to.

Shifting Gears

The year *preceding* my husband's death had been difficult because he had been quite sick for about seven months. I was missing the person that he had been. It was a very, very good marriage, and we had a lot of fun together, but that ended months before he died. He was angry at being sick and pulled into himself. He wanted me to somehow make him better, which I could not do.

A few years before, without going into much detail, his heart had been punctured by a pacemaker. He was in very, very serious condition. During his hospital stay, he held my hand, and he said, 'I know you won't let anything happen to me.' He couldn't ask this during his final illness. Near the end, he wouldn't even say good-bye because he was so upset. My husband's children felt very badly when he couldn't say good-bye; they felt my pain.

After his death, aside from the lack of companionship, which one would expect, things that my late husband did that were difficult for me to do, caught me off-guard. For instance, he had a wonderful sense of direction. So that whenever we went out, he would drive, and I never really had to learn exactly how to get any place.

I was not terribly lonely because I had books; I'm a "readaholic." I never even felt the emptiness of the house; my books were always waiting for me. It was a sort of nesting in and just taking care of myself with my books, a re-nourishing of myself as opposed to feeling scared or feeling that I couldn't function alone.

Plato Did It

A year after his death I joined the Plato Society, which is a study group through UCLA Extension, but a separate organization where we meet and teach active courses. I accepted an invitation to a new members' party exactly one year after my husband had died, and for the first time, I took off my wedding ring before leaving the house. It was at this party that Richard and I casually met.

I hadn't thought of meeting people by joining the Plato Society. The Society is a very demanding type of place, so you join because you want the intellectual stimulation. But I felt I needed to meet some other women and start doing things with them because my other women friends were all married, and I hoped to find someone to travel with. The idea of meeting a man sounded nice if it happened, but that wasn't a goal. There usually are more women around than men anyway, and I didn't even think of dating, though if it happened, that would be fine.

The following Thursday there was a new-member luncheon, to talk about the classes we had been in, and Richard was there. We happened to walk in together. He called me that evening and we have been seeing each other ever since.

The first evening that Richard and I went out, we went to dinner. When he brought me home, he casually asked, "Do you like dogs?" I answered, "Yes, but I wouldn't want to own one because it really ties you down. If you go any place overnight, the dog has to go to a kennel, and if you go away for a few days, the dog has a motel bill." He didn't say another word about 'a dog' after that. Soon enough I came to learn that Richard not only has a dog, but it's not even a cuddly dog. She doesn't sit on your lap; she sits or leans on your chest. It's a nice dog, but it hasn't added to the relationship.

Ready, Set, Go
Richard and I became romantically involved right away. It was just sort of a natural process. But yet, it was alarming. I said to Richard, 'You know, I haven't dated anyone since my husband died.' It was obvious that we were getting close very quickly. Even our first two hours together were comfortable because Richard is so comfortable. His answer? 'If you'd like to go out with nine other guys, I can

wait here for a while, while you do that. And then, maybe, you know, you'll come back and choose me.' But since he wasn't going to supply the nine other guys, it didn't work out that way.

People who knew my husband say he and Richard are opposites, and in many ways they are. In fact, both of my former husbands were very strong and controlling, and Richard is not. He is the first person I've been with who is very loving but in a non-demanding way. He appreciates who I am so that our relationship is very warm and easy, which is very new for me.

The other side to this is that my deceased husband has become a big part of our lives. I get to talk about him as much as I would like to, about our adventures, what he was like, our travels, etc. Being able to share this lets me be close to my husband *and* brings me closer to Richard, it's like they're both part of the family.

A New Song

Richard is not controlling or critical of me. My two husbands were, and I am able to bask in the knowing that someone really cares and appreciates me for who I am. I feel the same way about Richard; we absolutely bask in each other's approval and appreciation.

My late husband was an adventurer, which I loved and wouldn't have given up. We climbed through caves in Borneo and had a very adventuresome life. Richard and I have not traveled, and I have finally recognized that while Richard would be happy to go any place I want to go, he would be just as happy not to go anywhere. It's such an odd concept to me that it took me a long time to actually digest it.

This was a good time to have met Richard. One of the things he's taught me to do is shop. I am a very, very big non-shopper. When we met, I tended to wear clothes from the Gap, a T-shirt and jeans. Now I shop at Chico's.

I've always been a wanderer. When Richard and I wander together, we'll look for artwork. Because we live in my house, Richard enjoys adding artwork to make it more 'our house.' His shopping interests and my wandering interests combine well. We also go to the theater and movies and go out with friends. But, we do have more fun when we're out just the two of us.

In the mornings, particularly, if we don't have an appointment, we lounge around before we get up. Just talking about, you know, all the ideas that we have. We talk about what the kids are doing, what the grandkids are doing. I have six grandchildren, now eight including Richard's. Richard has become everyone's grandpa. That has become very special too because my grandchildren lost a grandpa, but have gained a new one.

Whenever we talk, it's as if we're not exactly meeting for the first time, but there's always the excitement of comparing views and telling each other about things. And one of the things that is most important to me in the relationship, is that when you love somebody, you want to tell them what's going on, and hear what's going on with them.

Like Falling Off a Log

Being intimate, and vulnerable was easy, not scary at all. It was a very nice thing to have sex back in my life. It was not only a big plus in our relationship, but a very major part of the relationship as it developed.

I had had two husbands already. My expectation was to just have a nice sex life, which is what happened. We were both very, very natural and easy-going about getting involved sexually. I guess partly I've always been young for my age, like somewhere between 6 and 25 or something. So we live life as if we were kids just discovering the world together. And since we both have the same attitude, it makes life very exciting and fun—he calls me his "Phi Beta Poopsie."

Oops!

There wasn't really a bump to be overcome, so much as a "confusion." When we met, Richard was living in an apartment and kept it even when he began staying most of the time at my house. I had a house and an established life and he was joining me in it, and though he didn't seem in any way like an opportunist, I had this small feeling of "Is this wonderful, loving man, the world's best con artist?" I was gaining a wonderful man, but he was gaining, in addition to a mate, a different lifestyle. And that, I was a little scared about.

Finally, after he hadn't been in his apartment for a few months, his landlady approached him and asked, though his lease was not up, if he wanted her to rent it. He did, and she did, and we were finally really living together.

No Regrets

There's nothing I would have done differently. And my family was supportive. It was a little startling that I was with Richard since I had not dated or even tried to meet anybody. Before Richard, even one of my stepdaughters tried to fix me up, or suggested I try meeting someone through the Internet. She was concerned. So, when Richard and I happened so fast, it probably felt a little funny to her. She even asked, "Are you going to give him the house?" To which I answered, "No, I have my five children in the will."

Richard and I aren't interested in prenuptials or any kind of legal agreement, which is one of the reasons we're not married. Were we to marry, I just feel that rather than a religious person or a judge, we would be dealing mostly with a lawyer, so it seems easier just to keep it this way. We hope to have many years, at least 20, of good health and togetherness.

Because I never tried to meet someone, I have no advice to offer on that front. It was just one of those things that happen and since he was so comfortable to be with, I could see us being together forever. He was just so—easy. So many women that I know would love to meet people and I don't know how you go about doing that, because I wasn't trying and it just happened. But I will say that it's important to know that it's OK to be happy again after bereavement.

You are not hurting your late spouse, in fact, if you had a good marriage, you will know how to be happy in a new relationship, if you allow yourself to be. You don't owe it to your deceased spouse to stay miserable. Hopefully, if you're open, maybe you can have another relationship that will add a great deal to your life.

Richard

I got married the first time at 38 to a woman I can't say I was madly in love with. I admired her, respected her and thought she'd make a good wife and mother, which she did. We had two children. She was an artist, art teacher, and drama queen—everything was a big deal to her. We had our problems but it was a decent marriage for 20 years. We separated when my younger son had graduated from high school and his brother, a year and a half older, was out on his own.

My second wife was a tough person, a businesswoman. She was tough on me. We were not a good match. She had been a widow for about six years and our getting together was kind of like storybook stuff. She died, after a five-year ordeal, of cancer.

After my wife's death, I had little or almost no support, from her family. But my two sons, who were living locally at the time, even though they didn't like her because they knew it had not been a good marriage and were resentful of her, gave me a certain amount of support.

My best support was professional, and the support from PLATO, which I had joined a couple of years prior to her passing helped, including the PLATO "casserole ladies." Nothing romantic, but we had little outside movie groups, studies and once, a little dinner party for me.

I went to a grief support group meeting one time. My wife's son's mother-in-law died a couple of days before, so I went with his father-in-law, who was grieving. I couldn't relate to the other members of the group.

I then went to another bereavement support group, also once. After the meeting, the woman in charge turned to me and said, "You don't belong here," which was obvious to me. I wasn't like everyone else. She suggested that I go to a therapist who I'd met with five or six times just to have someone to talk to. I realize that I'm not your typical mourner. I just wanted to know what my grief should be and how I should grieve. Should I feel guilty? I know that given the circumstance of my wife's death, I did all a person could and should have done. But the reality was that it was almost a relief when I became a widower. I was sorry for my wife's death, but not grieving, per se, because I was out of a bad marriage. The big question I needed to work out in therapy was, why hadn't I left the marriage years before? I still cannot answer that question.

A Door Opens

I didn't waste any time before dating again. It happened early on; maybe a month after my wife's passing. Loneliness, a hope of friendship and the wish for physical intimacy all played a role in my decision to date.

I don't like to be alone, so I did enjoy going out with people and enjoyed nice conversations. I had been single a long time before and between marriages and probably dated more than the average person who gets married in their 20s, but yes, I was looking for companionship. As far as a physical relationship, there has to be that 'spark' or 'chemistry.' And yes, I was lonely, but again, I was lonely in my marriage.

I met Tobie at a party for new members of an organization I belonged to. I met her and we chatted for a minute or so with a few other people. And I thought, "Hey, she's nice." That was a Sunday. The following Thursday, as Tobie said, we both walked into this room where we were going to attend a luncheon. I happened to sit next to her, and we chatted. Afterwards I gave her a little time to get home and then, about three o'clock, I called and said, 'If you're not busy for dinner, I'll be there at 6.'

She had just had a cataract operation the day before so she said, 'As long as I don't to have to get dressed up in anything fancy.' I said no, and we went out. Actually, we sat and talked in her living room first and then went out to dinner, and, as they say, the rest is history. Although I have never put the words 'soul mate' into my vocabulary, I just think Tobie and I are soul mates.

Though we were hardly friends when we became romantically involved, sex certainly helped to cement the relationship.

If anything, this new relationship underscored what I had been missing before. I see the differences, perhaps negatively in a sense. My late wife was a very successful, much respected businesswoman. But she was tough. With Tobie, not only do I love her deeply, but I admire her, including her intellect. She doesn't always come on strong, but I've learned to sit back and listen to her because she's usually right. And I'm not threatened with that at all.

I also admire her sense of adventure and her friendliness. She's had three stepchildren for 36 years, and they are almost like her biological children. She has a step-son-in-law who calls her more than one of my sons calls me—she's just wonderful. Everyone who meets her sees her genuineness and warmth. She's very friendly and smart as hell. Tobie also has a tremendous amount of empathy for people. Her academic success has been very great. She's extremely warm, touchy-feely, which I love. Very sexual. Very open. She's that combination of brains and sensuality which always turns me on. I love the intellectual wild-girl type.

Tobie is also so completely accepting, not critical or judgmental. We can talk though any problem; it's just a matter of sitting down and laying it out. I appreciated this ability so much; I never had that. And we both appreciate each other and what we've brought to each other's life. It's been wonderful, something I never, ever expected to find.

Opening Up

I never felt vulnerable with Tobie. After all those years of dating, my two marriages, and the way I'm able to open up with Tobie, I feel that she has gotten the *best* Richard. And so we grew close in every way.

Before Tobie, I had wondered, will I ever have that again or remember how to – but it's very natural. No problem. Nothing scary.

That's another thing about Tobie. She's so open and uncritical that any little problems, we just worked them out. She's made me into the best person I've ever been. That's the way she is. I didn't have any expectations other than to just see what happens. I've never tried to push, but you do sense when something is right.

Stuff Happens

Well, the only bump was, as Tobie said, when she questioned, was I the right person? She thought, He's practically moving in right away, and am I a rebound? I certainly understood that. But I sensed she was making the right decision for her. When I moved my dog in, that sort of finalized it. And then, when I put the doggy door in, that really said it all. I wouldn't change a thing that has happened, except for wishing that I had met Tobie sooner. My sons did not like my second wife, but they love Tobie.

We hope to be healthy and strong, to enjoy each other as long as we can.

My only advice to others is: Be open to new people.

Reflections

Richard and Tobie are genuinely happy that they have found each other, and appreciate each other greatly. They seem to come alive in the presence of each other. They both had been divorced as well as remarried. Now they have an opportunity to explore more learning and stimulation, which they revel in. They seem very compatible and comfortable. It is wonderful to watch them communicate and appreciate each other's worth.

The fact that Richard and Tobie had two other marriages, both unhappy, put them in a place to readily value what they have with each other. They particularly enjoy the intellectual stimulation they have between them, exemplified by their involvement in the PLATO Society. They seem very respectful of each other and appreciate that they have found each other, after suffering other hardships in other relationships.

For every beauty there is an eye somewhere to see it. For every truth there is an ear somewhere to hear it. For every love there is a heart somewhere to receive it.

Ivan Panin

12.

Nori & Charles

NORI IS AN attractive woman who looks much younger than her age. She is 77. She still works as a substitute teacher when needed. She is alert, articulate, sweet, giving and personable. Her late husband was in the furniture business. He died at 83 years of age, on Father's Day. She has a disabled son, a daughter who lives in France, and another son who lives here.

Charles is ninety-years-old, but you would never know it. He is bright, funny, involved and expressive. He is genuinely appreciative of Nori. Charles is very sparkly, enthusiastic and sweet. A typical example of Charles's kind nature was demonstrated when he recently joined Nori when she went to the cemetery to visit her late husband's grave. From what I've heard, he said, "I would have liked Irving because he was an honorable man. He would do business on a handshake. He always gave the other party the benefit of the doubt. Now-a-days, I don't see much of that at all."

Nori was married for almost 49 years; her late husband passed away four years ago. Charles was married twice, the first time for 52 years. His second marriage, which was unhappy, began two years later and lasted for eight. His first wife passed away 15 years ago, the second, three years ago.

Nori

When Irving died, I didn't have many friends in the city anymore. My best friend had moved out of town, but my family tried to be supportive despite obstacles. I have three children. My daughter lives in France, so she could not be of much help. I have a disabled son, who also was unable to be very supportive. My other son, his wife and children have been very helpful.

I attended a support group led by a local hospital, and then a different bereavement support group which I preferred. This group met weekly and I attended for two years after my husband's death.

Time helped my healing. I found at the beginning I was still crying a great deal. In fact, when I first started attending the group, I felt more depressed after the meetings than I had before. But I also think that I was healing. I believe it helped from two perspectives—being with others who understood the pain I was in helped, and it also helped when I was able to comfort others in the group who were in my same situation, or worse. I made friends and have continued to socialize with some of the group members after I no longer attended meetings.

The hardest period of time was at the beginning and then, when the season changed from summer to fall and then to winter and the days started getting shorter. That was difficult. My husband died in the summer and then the long winter nights began, and it got dark very early and it was very depressing. Driving home alone from my son's house, he lives a half-hour away, was difficult for me.

I tried to go to movies. I used to go to movies by myself all the time because my husband worked long late hours, but I couldn't go anymore. The hardest period of time was the first year, when I was so lonely. But the second year was also difficult when I fully realized how final the change in my life had really become.

A Change of Season

Charles and I began dating two years after my late husband's death. Actually, we didn't date, we 'met' during one of my final bereavement support group sessions. His wife died a year to the day after my husband, and he kind of 'wiggled' his way into my grief support group.

To tell you the truth, I was surprised by his invitation to dinner, but I went out with him and one thing just led to another. I never felt that I could be intimate again. I never felt that I could be attracted to another man and, to my surprise, it just happened. It started out as a friendship.

Our first date was funny because he asked me to dinner at a restaurant where the people from our bereavement support group got together before attending the weekly meeting. So we all sat together ... Charles took nine women to dinner. It was so funny. I had eight chaperones for our first date. He asked me out again for the following week, but I had plans to attend a wedding and a social function. I invited him to both and it worked out well. So, it started as a friendship and then it grew.

In Retrospect

This new relationship hasn't changed the way I think of my late husband or our marriage. I know there are similarities and many differences, but I am able to see that love exists in many different forms. I can love two different people in the same and different ways.

One small difference is that my late husband couldn't do anything mechanically. Charles is very mechanically inclined. Physically, their appearance is very different. They both have a wonderful sense of humor; my husband's was a little drier. They both are wonderful fathers. They were both wonderful husbands and very thoughtful. At this point in our lives, Charles is not as involved with business as my husband was in our furniture business, and then, after my husband retired, he spent most of his time at the card casino playing poker. My husband didn't believe much in exercise; Charles is at the gym three times a week. There is a big difference, yet many things are the same. They both love chocolate.

Because of their differences, I'm getting to appreciate things I never had experienced before – material and otherwise. Attention is one thing. Even my children say, "He gives you much more attention than Dad did." Charles is very kind, thoughtful, and generous. My husband was generous when he was able to be. They are both serious, but my late husband had a way of figuring that things would always be OK. He didn't plan ahead the way Charles did and does, including the way he has planned his life so that he has a nice old age.

Crossing Bridges

I did, however, rediscover old feelings when I allowed myself to become vulnerable again. It was flabbergasting. I just didn't expect it to happen and it happened. I felt like a teenager. On our first date, I felt silly getting in the car. And, what do you say? I wondered, how come I'm second-guessing myself? I'm not 16!

It was all a little bit scary, but not terribly because I figured, what the heck do I have to lose at 75 years old? And that same attitude continued when we became physically intimate.

It just happened. It was pleasant, it wasn't scary.

Even confronting today's expectations of sexuality didn't faze me. To tell you the truth, today we *are* like the kids. They live together without being married; so do we. Except that recently his kids moved into his house while they were remodeling theirs, so I didn't stay there during that time. But, they know we are together. They know we travel together. Charles has been married twice and is turning the corner on 90, but he doesn't look it. He's amazing!

I never really thought I would be sexually intimate ever again, I never even thought that I missed it, he just pressed the right buttons and I responded. Then I figured, I'll never see him again, he's probably thinking that something is wrong with me. So I think maybe the kids have it right. This kind of intimacy would never have happened years ago. When I was younger, I would never have been intimate without being married. But, I figured, what the heck. I'm not going to have children. We are both old enough and life is too short to waste.

Charles and I were able to talk about our expectations to some extent, which was something that hadn't happened in my marriage. My husband wasn't as comfortable talking about it as Charles and I are. I used to get undressed in the closet. It was just a different relationship. Now it's different. I don't undress in the closet.

No Potholes
There really weren't any major setbacks for us. Charles was seeing another woman only because he had promised to take her to the remaining shows from a series they had purchased tickets for. So when he mentioned it to me, I was glad because if my friends saw him out with somebody else, they would have told me and I would have felt terrible. He asked me to go camping with him, we just met in July and he wanted me to go away in his motor

home in September and I said, 'No, it's too soon.' So we went away in October.

As far as our relationship goes, I don't know if I would have done anything differently. My other bereavement support group members asked, 'Does he know about your son? Does he know about your eye?' I had a malignancy in my eye and have an emotionally disabled son, but I was honest right away, I didn't keep any secrets. And, thankfully, my eye is now fine.

Family Circle

We had absolutely no trouble with family, none at all. His family has been wonderful to me, they have gone beyond. They were so fabulous to me on my birthday and with spending holidays together. They are just very warm and loving and tell me how much more they like me than they did the last one – his second wife.

I hope we can go along like this for another five or 10 years; after all we are not very young. We don't expect to get married. He's helping me, but I am keeping my own home. He's asked me to move in with him and give up my condo, but I told him the truth about what I was thinking: 'If something happens to you, where will I go'? So it has been important to me to keep my condo.

Nori's Tips

Don't look too hard for someone. If it happens, it's going to happen. Let nature take its course. Looking back over my life, I sees my present happiness as a gift, in contrast to my early, difficult life. My mother left me as an infant and came back periodically. When I was five, she came back to stay, we thought, but she left again. We waited for her, but I didn't see her again until the day after my father's funeral, when I was nine. After I was pushed around the court system, my father's family took me in and I grew up with aunts and cousins, always like the stepchild. My father had provided for me, financially, thank goodness. I went away to college far away from the family. I started out as a social worker, and then became a teacher.

My marriage was very good. The last year and a half of his life, my late husband was in a wheelchair. I am reaping the reward now. I think that God is kind of paying me back for the problems I've had before. I'm happy now.

Charles

My three wonderful children were always there to help me with my grief, while at the same time; they hid their grief from me.

I also attended at grief support group for about three sessions. Unfortunately I found it difficult to relate to the other members and became annoyed when they didn't seem to be moving on in their grief, but just stayed stuck in sadness. Some of their tears annoyed me so I quit the group, and found that I felt a lot better. When my first wife died, my experience with a grief support group was very helpful, which was my reason for attending again when my second wife died. This time the experience was not positive. But I also believe that time is the best healer.

The most difficult thing was living in a huge, quiet house. The children would come over but they had their own lives to lead too.

Stepping Up

Before Nori and I got together, I went back to an activity I had previously enjoyed, square dancing. I met a woman there, but that didn't work out. So basically, at first I really didn't date. When I did begin going out, I was motivated by a need for friendship. I wasn't looking for anybody in particular. I just wanted companionship. Then I met Nori in the grief support group I'd attended briefly. We liked each other right away, that's all. She was easy to talk to and a lovely woman.

Letting Go of Anger

Truthfully, before I met Nori I had been very angry. After my second wife's death, looking back at that relationship, I felt that I had been used. There is no comparison between my second wife and Nori., but I do see similarities between Nori and my first wife. Both she and Nori are somewhat alike in both their temperament and attitude about life.

I appreciate the fact that I can talk with Nori while I couldn't do so with my second wife because she always had to be right.

Phase One

It wasn't scary for me at all to become emotionally vulnerable again. I was getting older and I noticed that I was much more talkative than I used to be. I went through four years of high school without ever saying a word. The teachers would always say, 'You are a joy to have around,' only because I never said anything. But, that doesn't keep me from thinking, and I'm more comfortable now expressing my sense of humor.

Phase Two

Exploring physical intimacy again was not scary at all. It was just natural. Frankly, I didn't give it much thought. It just happened, that's all ... and it was good, very good.

Although I would have felt comfortable talking about my expectations with Nori, we didn't do so. Things became more complicated when one of my grown children and their family moved back home while theirs were being remodeled, so Nori didn't stay over during that time. My kids still don't acknowledge that we sometimes sleep together. We know that they know but they don't talk about it."

Second Thoughts?

As far as Nori is concerned, there is nothing I would have done differently. We have been on trips that drew us closer to each other. Nori has a daughter in Paris, so we went to see her because she hadn't seen her daughter in a long time. While in Europe, we also visited Venice, Florence, and Rome. We went all over.

No Kidding

There were no problems with my family, no trouble spots at all. In fact it worked out very well. My youngest daughter is an aide for the public schools and Nori is a teacher, so they have a lot in common.

My hope is to live out the rest of our lives together, and either lie to each other or humor each other, which I say in jest. Really I just want to live out our lives living peacefully and happily.

My advice to others is basic, but not necessarily easy: Be honest with each other and keep your word. If you say you are going to do something, do it.

Reflections

Early in his loss, Charles couldn't tolerate the sadness of others. He went from group to group. He had trouble hearing about loss and wanted to feel better fast. He went to a group where he didn't have to address early pain. When he got there, he met Nori.

In their youth, cultural mores didn't provide Charles or Nori with an opportunity for self-expression or for talking about sex. But times changed, and many years later, Nori finds a partner she can talk to. There is a greater openness today, not only for verbal expression but for a shift in behavior. Nori and Charles would never have lived together years ago. They still are a bit shy about their children's knowing.

At 77 for Nori and 90 for Charles, they are enjoying a good life together with appreciation, care and love for one another. They travel together, are respectful and funny. When Charles tells a story differently than it happened, Nori injects the proper detail in a non-judgmental way. Charles tends to wander a bit in his details and Nori helps him get back on track and they are openly supportive of one another. Nori feels lucky that this relationship came her way and recognizes what a dividend for happiness, enjoyment and pleasure this is at their age.

Nori didn't expect another relationship. She is appreciative of Charles and supports him emotionally. Charles is openly supportive of her, too, and treats her like a treasure. He values her goodness and honesty.

He has a playful sense of humor and has explained his early grief in a direct and open way, sharing his story without pretense. He is a man who worked hard to build something for his family and he is very proud of his accomplishment. He is happy to share his good fortune with Nori and to enhance her life as well as his own. What a wonderful thing to see two people so happy and caring of each other—people who are a good example of moving from loss to love at any age.

13.

Love Life:
Sex as Grief Counselor
Jo Giese
The Los Angeles Times Magazine

A COUPLE OF YEARS AGO, my sister, who adored my husband yet understood he'd never recover, said to me, "If you took a lover, I wouldn't hold it against you. I probably wouldn't want to meet him, and if you tell anyone I said this, I'll deny it."

Where was this lover supposed to materialize? At the local coffee shop? I rarely left our Malibu neighborhood during my husband's illness—multi-infarct dementia, a disease related to Alzheimer's where the brain dies from multiple strokes. I pleaded with his doctor, "What is going on? Am I getting Douglas into tip-top physical shape only to give his brain a chance to die more? Then he won't recognize me or the dog?"

"Probably," said his doctor, who explained that Doug, who was also a doctor, could live another 10 years.

I thought about a friend whose father was dying in one part of the family home while her mother entertained a lover in another wing. The children never forgave her.

I didn't have children. I got a bikini wax.

I signed up at an Internet dating site. It wasn't until my first date spooned into his dessert that he asked the question I'd been dreading, "So, you're a widow?"

"Soon-to-be-widow."

"How soon?"

I wasn't ready for this. Even though my husband had that blank, thousand-mile stare, mouth gapping open, he was still lovely to me. Whenever I helped him—emptying is urinal, brushing his teeth—he thanked me. At least once a day he said, "You look beautiful, darling." No wonder I wasn't finished loving this man.

So it was a shock when the lover I'd been longing for turned up just 10 days after Douglas died. I found myself in that awkward initiation of one's youth. I was a 57-year-old virgin. After three years of celibacy, why hadn't any of my women friends warned me about this complication? And Hollywood didn't help, either. When Diane Keaton, a post-menopausal woman, takes Jack Nicholson as her lover in *Something's Gotta Give*, afterward she yells, "I love sex!" Me too, but—

Jim, a friend from Chicago, had come to the West Coast on business, and phoned. Before I met Douglas, Jim and I had been lovers—was hat 20 years ago? Jim had known Douglas, but didn't know that he'd just died. I asked if he'd like to come for dinner. He asked if I had a room where he could stay so he wouldn't have to drive back to Santa Barbara at night. I did.

In the first raw throes of grieving, nightfall delivered a shock of grief so black it was dangerous to be alone. "The sunset's lovely from the deck. Come before dark."

I can understand how it could seem otherwise, but I was paralyzed with grief when I invited Jim to dinner. If I'd had any idea his visit would lead to something more, I wouldn't have been wearing frumpy sweats when he arrived. It was a warm February evening, the sliding glass doors to the deck were open wide, and the tide was out as I showed Jim around our beach house—it was too soon to say "my" beach house. Years ago, this tall Chinese man wore a hippie ponytail; now 55, his graying hair was trimmed short, Dalai Lama style. It was a joy to see that he still had an easy laugh, a warm smile.

He put on a CD of old standards that he brought, starting with, of all things, Patsy Cline's "I Fall to Pieces." I poured us some Chardonnay. I told him that for the past 13 months Douglas had slept there—across from the couch in a hospital bed, rails up—and how I or one of his professional caregivers had slept near him, here on the couch in the living room where we were sitting.

Now "Georgia on my Mind" was playing. Jim extended a hand. "Let's dance," he said. Because the rugs had been taken up to make the floors wheelchair smooth, they were perfect for dancing. To move again, to dance in the very room that had held such illness, was a miracle. And to have an old friend, who was single, turn up at such a time was a gift from the universe.

"I like to kiss," he reminded me, extending a further invitation.

I ordered dinner in.

Was this too soon? Was this disrespectful? A friend whose husband had just died thought my timing was perfect: "This is anti-Death. This is what one does being fully alive instead of tiptoeing around Death."

Upstairs in bed, there was a softening, an opening up, opening out, life expressing itself again.

"You're like a 17-year-old kid," Jim said.

Here's where the "virgin" part comes in: Fifty-seven going on 17, my body had tightened up, and I was reduced to that embarrassing situation where the boy can do anything ... anything but *that*. Maybe it was okay that we had to go slowly, carefully. Maybe this was nature's awareness about the amount of intimacy I could handle.

Jim didn't leave the next day. Or the next. His next assignment—he's a diversity trainer for major corporations—was postponed and he ended up staying 23 nights. Each evening we danced. He would twirl me out and swing me back in. Other times we held each other and swayed, slow dancing. This was dance as foreplay, as therapy. I never expected that, in between grief seizures, life could feel like heaven on earth.

One morning, while still in bed, he said, "You're frisky today."

"Thanks to you!"

As we reached out to each other, he noticed something sticking to his back. I pulled off a small brown wad. And smelled it. Oh, God, an offering from Charmlee, my three-year-old Yorkie.

"A *turd!*" Jim said, getting the heebie jeebies, as anybody would, and I didn't blame him.

We still wanted to make love, but we were laughing too hard. Each time we started—"A *turd* was on my back!"—we burst out laughing again. There's kinky sex, boring sex, passionate sex, but not funny sex. It's not possible to make love and laugh that hard at the same time.

"Good grief," I said to Jim, "where's my grief gone?"

Was I laughing and dancing and making-love instead of grieving? Damn straight.

Jim didn't do away with my grief. He was an island to pull up on, a respite from the crashing waves. Because even with my lover in the house, grief still took its bite. Anything—a glimpse of Douglas' handsome face in his obituary photo—could set it off.

"You're not my grief counselor," I reminded him, as he held me. But in a way, a good way, he was, and we both knew it.

It was a dreamy time in which I, a madrigal, who usually flies out of bed at six, slept in until ten. I served Jim coffee; he made me breakfast. I limited myself to two condolence calls a day; voice mail caught the rest. We hiked in the Santa Monica Mountains and watched the clouds float across the sky.

If I'd been younger and had swooned on this cloud of love with a man, I probably would have been rushing to plan a future. Now I had no expectations beyond this present moment. Besides, Jim had never married—commitment was not this man's middle name. He was a hummingbird, forever visiting the flowers, always moving on.

One morning, raising his head on the pillow, he asked, "Were you upset with me last night? When I came upstairs, you were asleep."

In a recent relationship, he explained, sometimes his partner had turned her back to him and gone to bed angry.

"Douglas and I had no time for that," I said, explaining that I was just tired. "We knew life was too short."

I understood the gift of reawakening Jim had given me; I hadn't understood the gift I'd given him. I was learning that Jim, or any man I would be with in the future, was the lucky beneficiary of my having had a lovely, easy relationship for 17 years. To turn away from your beloved, to waste a single night in anger—that's the luxury of the young.

I'm still living that lesson a year later. A new friend just described my ability to extract the most from every day as dazzling. Exactly. When you watch someone die in your living-room, you learn life is for the living. Today.

Jo Giese is a special correspondent at "Marketplace," public radio's daily business program, and a contributor to "This American Life." She is working on "A Starbucks Romance," a memoir.

Jo Giese 31500 Broad Beach Road, Malibu, California, 90265 - 310-457-0624 jogiese@charter.net/Reprinted with Permission, Jo Giese & MSReprints

14.

Bringing It All Together

YOU HAVE READ OUR stories of love and stores of resolve; men and women determined to go on, to create fulfilling new lives following their heartbreaking loss, people willing to trust again, people willing to transcend the loss of their spouse to new love. Perhaps this begs the question: *How* were these people able to overlap their grieving and their loving?

For the most part, the widows and widowers you have met joined and stayed in their bereavement support groups; they continued to get group support and feedback during their mourning. They were able to question, share and feel less isolated in their grief, to talk to each other about their feelings. Although, not everyone can tolerate the deep introspection that a bereavement support group promotes, particularly the men.

For the widow and widower, there was a certain degree of comfort in dating other widows and widowers. Not only could they understand, but could tolerate conversations with each other about their late spouses.

They felt "safe" with each other and experienced a type of "comfort" level with each other as a result of a common experience.

Can you really love again before you have fully grieved? At first people might want the security blanket of a "friendship" – without strings. But, many of the men and women you've just met described a progression from friendship to physical and emotional attachment.

Timing seems to be a crucial factor in that if people start to date early on, it is harder to understand and separate our feelings, i.e., "Do I really have genuine caring feelings for this person?" or, "Is he/she taking away my pain of loneliness?" Or, if the man has a lot of money, the woman might have difficulty sifting out, "Do I care about him because he could make my life easier?" "Would I have strong feelings for him if he didn't have money?" Perhaps the underlying question is: "Is it possible to fall in love with a new partner while you are still mourning your first love?"

In *The Healing Power of Grief*, our goal was to explore how people grieve, mourn and move on to new successful relationships. We found that the answer lies in time and the willingness to face our grief versus hiding. It takes time to grieve, to reflect and reveal the inner pain. While in the company of another person of the opposite sex who has had the same experience, it often becomes easier to share and talk of the deceased. The world is safer. The new friend understands differently than married friends and the people who have not experienced spousal loss. In a climate of acceptance and warmth, new love is allowed to flourish. The outside world is not always tolerant of your normal need to tell your story over and over again.

We also found that when people had a solid connection with their late spouse and a happy marriage, they wanted that connection again. Men seemed to have less interest in wanting to be alone; women seemed to move more slowly in their expression of loss. They often had girlfriends to talk to who understood. The men we talked to wanted a connection with a woman. The female might have wanted to be connected again too, but seemed more fearful.

When it did happen, when people overcame their insecurities and their doubts and met and began to blend their life with another's, it was exhilarating and satisfying. It was happy. It was not without its troubles or difficulties but in the second half of life, it was so appreciated. People voiced that they were delighted to meet another meaningful partner, to have a life that was less alone, to have company to enjoy all that life has to offer.

All exhibited an attitude of gratefulness for finding a soul that might be a soul-mate, or at least a wonderful companion. And so, what transcended aging, was a spirit of adventure and joy and pleasure that life could be good again. Most saw their meeting as an opportunity for happiness, for long term goals — regardless of age — to enjoy good health, to share life and to transcend grief into new love.

Love puts the fun in together,
The sad in apart,
The hope in tomorrow,
The joy in the heart.
Anonymous

About the Authors

Gloria Lintermans

Los Angeles-based **Gloria Lintermans** is a widow, freelance writer and former internationally syndicated columnist; her column appeared in English and Spanish language newspapers across the U.S. from Hawaii to New York and worldwide from Saudi Arabia to South America.

Lintermans has authored: *CHEAP CHIC: A Guide to LA's Resale Boutiques* (1990), the "ultimate guide to recycled fashion," and forerunner of *RETRO CHIC: A Guide to Fabulous Vintage and Designer Resale Shopping in North America & Online* (Really Great Books, Los Angeles, 2002); *The Newly Divorced Book of Protocol* (Barricade Books, New York, 1995), and *The Healing Power of Grief* (Champion Press, 2006) co-authored by Dr. Marilyn Stolzman. Lintermans has also written for numerous national and local magazines.

Lintermans has appeared on radio and television talk shows across the country including: the "Donna Mason Show," Raleigh, NC; "Steve Kalk Show," Beaver Falls, PA; "Morning Drive with John Dawson," Albany, GA; "Tim Quinn Show," Bridgeport, CT, "What You Should Know About," Philadelphia, PA; "Memphis in the Morning," Memphis, TN; "Kent Slocum Show," Grand Rapids, MI; "The Michael Jackson Show," Los Angeles, CA, among others. She has hosted her own "Looking

Great with Gloria Lintermans" cable television and radio shows and is a popular lecturer and commentator.

Lintermans is a member of The Authors Guild, Inc., the National Society of Newspaper Columnists and A.F.T.R.A. (American Federation of Television & Radio Artists). Lintermans lives in Los Angeles.

Lintermans is a widow whose experience of loss and new love has become the basis for *THE HEALING POWER OF GRIEF: The Journey Through Loss to Life and Laughter* and *THE HEALING POWER OF LOVE: Transcending the Loss of a Spouse to New Love,* each co-authored by Dr. Marilyn Stolzman.

Dr. Marilyn Stolzman

Drawn to the healing aspect of grief counseling, Los Angeles-based **Dr. Marilyn Stolzman** became a professional counselor specializing in bereavement. After acquiring her hospice training, an internship at the American Cancer Society, and her L.M.F.T. license, Dr. Stolzman was hired and trained by the head of social services at Encino Hospital in Southern California to lead their hospital's bereavement program; at that point, she had been a practicing therapist for a year and had started a cancer support group for women in 1973 at the Mid-Westchester YWCA in Scarsdale, NY. Dr. Stolzman is a certified clinical Hypnotherapist. She is a popular lecturer and has lectured for The American Institute of Medical Education in France, Hawaii, Santa Fe and Hong Kong.

She has also been a frequent lecturer at The Oaks in Ojai, CA, Kaiser Permanente, and Pierce College, Woodland Hills, CA.

She has taught bereavement classes at the Phillips Graduate Institute in Southern California, and for doctorate students at Ryokan College in Venice, CA. She has taught Continuing Education classes at California State University Northridge and at Encino-Tarzana Regional Medical Center. She is completing a book on Hypnosis with colleague Trudy Moss, Ph.D.

Currently, Dr. Stolzman directs the Southern California bereavement and transition support program, H.O.P.E. UNIT FOUNDATION, which offers a life-affirming two-year support group program. The literature supports that people do 50 percent better if they attend a bereavement group, and this is how Dr. Stolzman sums it up:

A bereavement support group helps people to "normalize" feelings and receive validation and feedback from each other and from the therapists. People know they are not alone, not isolated. Group support makes people recognize that they are not going crazy. There is comfort in knowing that others feel the same way. Everyone goes through their grieving differently depending on their own ego strengths, their history, their coping strategies and their life experience. A support group needs to provide a safe, warm atmosphere where people can trust that what they share is contained and stays in the group. It is important for the group to be led by licensed professionals.

This experience led to **THE HEALING POWER OF GRIEF:** *The Journey Through Loss to Life and Laughter* and **THE HEALING POWER OF LOVE:** *Transcending the Loss of a Spouse to New Love*, each co-authored by Gloria Lintermans.

THE HEALING POWER OF GRIEF
The Journey Through Loss to Life and Laughter
by Gloria Lintermans & Marilyn Stolzman, Ph.D.,
L.M.F.T., Champion Press

AS THE SAYING GOES, there are only two things unavoidable in life: taxes and dying. Along with dying there is, more often than not, a spouse or life-partner left to grieve. These bereft partners are our concern. Why are some able to heal and eventually experience a fulfilling new life, while others wither emotionally, spiritually, and even physically, never fully recovering from their loss? When losing a spouse is so common, why do we need a blueprint to overcome our suffering and eventually, achieve healing? Why is *healthy* mourning, as opposed to a prolonged state of emotional denial important in creating a rewarding new life?

Facing such a loss head on *is difficult* because loving is all-encompassing; love took most of our emotional energy as we embraced our spouse or partner. We cared that they were fulfilled and well. We wanted to protect them and make them happy. We were devoted, so much so, that losing this loved one, felt crippling. And so, when they are gone, we need to learn how to transform this energy into something positive. Not a "substitute," but a conversion, from a "we" to an "I." Not in a selfish manner, but as a way of refocusing, we ask "How do I live my life in a positive way without you ... *not* losing the memory and loving feelings of you, but incorporating them and going on? What tools can I find? How do I learn to heal in a way that's positive and energizing instead of depleting?"

THE HEALING POWER OF GRIEF is Gloria Lintermans' story, twenty-four months of mourning and healing following the death of her precious husband, Rick. It is also Dr. Marilyn Stolzman's, a psychotherapist specializing in grief counseling, vision of healing as she offers tools, not psychobabble, a blueprint as it were, to help you to face your loss, mourn, and eventually, heal.

Together, they share their experiences as they take you gently by the hand to give you comfort and direction during this confusing and painful time. It has been shown that the *only* way to arrive at a healthy, *healed* integration, adjustment and transition is by going through the shock, denial, envy, anger, depression and guilt that the loss of a spouse predictably inspires. It is important to note that these stages are based loosely on the "stages of grief" first acknowledged by Dr. Elizabeth Kubler-Ross for those "living while dying."

Unlike any other book, **THE HEALING POWER OF GRIEF** is based on the *Time Sequences of Grief.* Chapter-by-chapter, chapters one to five represent a time sequence divided by months of mourning. Each includes a first-hand account of mourning; answers to commonly asked questions concerning your day-to-day life; Dr. Stolzman's reassuring explanation of what you are feeling; a roadmap of helpful Do's and Don'ts to guide you and your support community on your path to recovery; help, specific to the LGBT Community; and a Healing Power of

Thought Workbook to assist the bereaved with their expression and resolution of painful feelings.